Spiritual War

DECREEING

YOUR

HEALING

Kenneth Scott

Unless otherwise noted, all scriptures in this publication are taken from the King James version of the Bible, or paraphrased by the author.

Decreeing Your Healing
P7C

Copyright © 2016 by Kenneth Scott
Spiritual Warfare Ministries, Inc.
P.O. Box 2024
Birmingham, AL 35201-2024
(205) 853-9509

All rights reserved. Contents and/or cover of this book may not be reproduced or transmitted in any form or by any means, electronically or mechanically, without written permission from the author and publisher.

To request written permission to reproduce sections of this publication, contact us at:

Spiritual Warfare Ministries
Attention: Kenneth Scott
P.O. Box 2024
Birmingham, Alabama 35201-2024
(205) 853-9509

www.prayerwarfare.com

email us at prayerbooks@aol.com

Thou shalt also decree a thing, and it shall be established unto thee: and the light shall shine upon thy ways.
Job 22:28

Contents

Introduction 6

Taking the Medicine of God's Word 9

Jesus, the Antidote for Our Sickness and Diseases .. 19

Healing Through His Sufferings 27

A Picture of Our Healing in the Passover 39

Instructions on How to Take Holy Communion 45

Is Healing Just for the Righteous? 51

Things That Hinder Our Healing 57

Spiritual Warfare Prayer over Your Body 65

Introduction to Warfare Healing Confessions 69

Spiritual Warfare Healing Confessions 71

Introduction

In Job 22:18, the Bible says, *"thou shalt also decree a thing, and it shall be established unto thee: and the light shall shine upon thy ways."* Many are praying and asking God to heal them, but God is saying that He is waiting for us to use the keys He has given unto us to decree and declare our healing; then our healing shall be established.

In the first part of this book, you will find several chapters that will help you to understand God's divine plan of healing for you. It will give you the knowledge, understanding, and confidence to know that you have a God-given, Christ-sacrificed, blood-bought right to be healed.

The second part of this book includes 160 scriptural spiritual warfare healing confessions. They are powerful keys that will aid and assist you in unlocking the door to your divine healing.

The Bible tells us in Romans 12:2 that we become transformed by the Word of God. As you utilize these powerful keys of spiritual warfare healing confessions over your life and body, you will begin to see and experience the manifestation and transformation in your body from sickness and disease to healing, wellness, and wholeness.

These powerful healing keys are not just for those who are looking to be healed; they are also for those who want to maintain their healing.

Now, get ready to experience another dimension in spiritual warfare of God's power and deliverance in your health and your body as you use these powerful keys, to ***"Decree your Healing."***

Chapter 1

Taking the Medicine of God's Word

As we begin to study and understand God's divine plan for our healing, we want to begin by understanding God's process of using His Word as medicine for us. Just as God has blessed us with medicine to help our bodies to recover, God has more abundantly designed His Word as a type of spiritual medicine that (if used correctly) will heal our whole being—spirit, soul, and body. Now, let us begin by exploring God's Word as our healing balm.

> *My son, attend to my words; incline thine ear unto my sayings. Let them not depart from thine eyes; keep them in the midst of thine heart. For they are life unto those that find them, and health to all their flesh. (Pro 4:20-22)*

In this passage, God tells us that His Word will bring us health and healing. The Hebrew word for *"health"* in this passage is actually the word *"medicine."* God is telling us that His Word is like healing medicine to us. As we already know, medicine will not work unless you take it properly.

So we must learn how to properly take the medicine of God's Word in order for it to be effective in healing our bodies.

In this chapter, we will use six points of instructions in comparing how we usually take physical medicine to how we are to take the spiritual medicine of God's Word. And just as we can get healed from listening to a physical doctor and properly take the medicine he prescribes, we can even more abundantly receive our divine healing from God if we listen to His instructions and properly take His prescribed medicine.

These instructions are as follows:

1. Pay Attention to the Doctor's Instructions

My son, attend to my words; incline thine ear unto my sayings. (Pro 4:20-22)

God starts off His instructions by telling us to *"attend"* to His Word. This word *"attend"* can be compared to an *"attending"* physician. In a hospital, the head physician is called the *"attending"* physician. He is considered the head doctor. He is the one who unlimitedly determines your treatment and gives directions for your care.

The attending doctor not only gives instructions to the other doctors, he also gives instructions to the patient. If a patient wants to get well, they must be careful to listen to the words of the attending doctor.

When the attending physician comes in the room, someone usually *inclines* the patient's bed *(incline thine ear to my sayings...)* so that the patient can sit up and pay close and careful attention to the instructions of the attending doctor.

Imagine a situation were you are in the hospital, and the attending physician along with his other doctors come into your room. They *incline* your bed so that you can sit up and attentively hear what the *attending* doctor is saying.

The attending doctor then begins to speak.

As he speaks, you pay close attention to what he says. He tells you that you are going to be fine and recover, provided that you follow His instructions and take the medicine He is prescribing for you correctly.

Spiritually, God is our attending doctor. He is giving instructions for us to *attend* to, just as we would do to the *attending* doctor. And just as a patient can get well if they take the medicine and follow the attending doctor's instructions, we can also be healed if we are willing to listen to the instructions of our attending doctor (God) and take His prescribed medicine (the Word of God) as directed.

2. You Must Believe the Medicine Will Work

Therefore I say unto you, What things soever ye desire, when ye pray, believe that ye receive them, and ye shall have them. (Mark 11:24)

God has created the natural seed to grow and produce. He has instilled everything within the seed to grow and become plants and trees to produce fruit. Two important things God requires for the seed to grow are soil and water. Everything else the seed needs to grow and produce fruit is supernaturally provided by God.

God has also instilled within the seed of His Word everything it needs to grow and produce the fruit of your healing, blessings, and whatever you need. But just as you must have water and soil for the natural seed to produce, you must also have spiritual soil and water for the seed of God's Word to produce your need.

For unto us was the gospel preached, as well as unto them: but the word preached did not profit them, not being mixed with faith in them that heard it. (Heb 4:2)

This passage shows us that some people will prosper

from the Word of God, and some will not prosper. The reason some will not prosper is because they will not mix the Word of God with faith. Spiritually, the soil is your fertile heart to receive the Word, and the water is represented by your faith. The seed of God's Word needs your faith to grow and produce in your life. You must believe and know that God put everything you need concerning your healing in His Word. And as you plant it in your heart with reading and confessing His Word concerning your healing, and properly watering it with your faith, it is going to germinate, grow, and produce your healing.

3. Don't Take Expired Medicine

When you take physical medicine, you must be careful not to take medicine that is expired. Expired medicine loses its potency and becomes ineffective in treating and helping you. In addition to that, it can also harm you. Just as you must not take expired (physical) medicine, you must also be careful to make sure that you take current *"spiritual"* medicine that is not expired.

Now Faith

> *Now faith is the substance of things hoped for, the evidence of things not seen. (Heb 11:1)*

Notice it says, **"Now Faith..."** Just like your physical medicine, your faith must also be current (now faith). Faith does not come because you heard something that provoked faith in your heart in the past, it comes when you have a *"now"* or current and active freshness of your faith.

For example: Let's say that you needed healing six months ago and you got into the Word and read and confessed the Word and received your healing. But let's say that six months later you became afflicted with something else and needed healing again. You cannot rely on the

Word that you feasted off of six months ago to receive your current healing. You would need to go and get back into the Word again to get a fresh dose of faith that comes as a result of hearing a fresh Word of God to give you fresh faith to believe and receive. *(Rom 10:10).*

In Exodus chapters 15 and 16, God delivered the children of Israel out of Egypt and brought them across the Red Sea on dry land. Shortly afterwards, they began to murmur and complain about not having food, so God sent them manna (bread from heaven). God had given specific instructions for Moses to give the people regarding the manna. When the manna fell, they were only to get enough for each member of the household and only for the current day. As expected, there were many that ignored God's instructions and attempted to stockpile extra for the next day. Those who disobeyed God found that when they awakened the next morning, the extra manna they tried to save had turned into worms and began to stink profusely.

The same manna that was a blessing to them a day earlier was now stinking. The same thing happens to physical medicine. Again, the same medicine that once helped a person can harm them if they take it after it expires.

> *But my horn shalt thou exalt like the horn of an unicorn: I shall be anointed with fresh oil. (Ps 92:10)*

In this passage, the horn represents health and strength. So God is saying that we will get renewed strength (and healing) when we get the freshness of His anointing. We get the anointing when we get into the presence of God through hearing, speaking, and confessing the Word of God.

Whether you are a pastor, bishop, or anyone else, if you need God to move for you, it doesn't matter how much of the Bible you know or how many scriptures you can quote, you still have to go and get a fresh dose of the Word.

I tell people that when you need God to move on your behalf, act like you have never read or heard anything in the Bible before. Go and listen to and speak the Word daily like it is brand new to you. When you do this, you will receive the freshness of God's anointing upon that Word to receive your healing.

While you are in need of healing, take a dose of the Word concerning your healing each and every day. In fact, take it like physical medicine—several times a day. Remember, our initial scripture says that God's Word is like medicine. So you need to take it like medicine—every day, several times a day. And just as the natural seed mixes with soil and water and produces fruit, when you mix your (daily, fresh) faith with reading and speaking the medicine of the Word of God, it will likewise produce the fruit of healing in your life.

4. God's Medicine Must Be Taken Internally

Medicine must be taken and applied as directed. Some medicines are topical; meaning, that you apply it on the outside of your skin. Some are injectable—to be injected with a needle and syringe. Most, however, are internal—to be taken orally. If you fail to apply the medicine according to the directions, it will not work.

...keep them in the midst of thine heart. (Pro 4:21)

Just as with most medicines, the application of God's Word is always oral and internal. It's oral because you have to read and speak (confess) it. It's internal because you have to get it in internally (inside your heart).

The medicine of God's Word cannot be applied topically. You must get it in you. The way we apply God's Word topically is to simply get His Word in our head. Just because you know what God's Word says does not mean that you have His Word in your heart. You could simply have His Word topically.

Just as internal medicines will not be effective if you apply them topically, the medicine of God's Word will not be effective if you only apply it topically.

Thy word have I hid in mine heart, that I might not sin against thee. (Ps 119:11)

In this passage David tells us the same thing. David said that in order for God's Word to be effective against sin, you must get it in your heart (take it internally). The other part of this passage also helps us to understand how we get it internally, which is to hide it. This word *"hide"* means to dig, as in digging to bury something. To dig a hole in order to bury something takes work. To just read it once or periodically read it is to use it topically. But in order to bury the Word of God in your heart, you need to do the work. This includes reading the Word, speaking and confessing the Word, meditating on the Word, and continuing to keep the Word in you. As you continue this cycle, the Word will migrate from your head and become planted in your heart where it will become manifested in the form of your healing.

5. You Must Not Skip Doses

Let them not depart from thine eyes.... (Pro 4:21)

The above passage tells us that we must not let the Word of God depart from our eyes. Another way of saying this is *"keep the medicine in your system."* When you take medicine, it stays in your system for a while before it dissipates. Some medicines stay for hours, some for days, and some even months. The way to maximize the effectiveness of the medicine and keep it in your system is to not skip doses.

Jesus tells us in *Matthew 6:11* that we should take a dose

of His Word daily (*our daily bread*) which is, by the way, the minimum recommended dosage. You can take the minimum dosage of the Word, but to get the full effectiveness of the Word, you take it as most oral medicines dictate, two or three times a day.

When you are believing God for your healing, you want the full effectiveness of God's Word. To do that, you keep it in your system by taking it at least two or three times a day. When you take God's Word like this, it will not have time to dissipate from your (spiritual) system. It will remain in your system and drive out the spirit of your infirmity.

6. You Must Give It Time to Work

For they are life unto those that find them, and health to all their flesh. (Pro 4:22)

The phrase *"For they are life..."* means that if we follow the principles of God's instructions, they *"will become"* life and healing. It's a process. Just as it takes time for natural medicine to work, it also takes time to receive the healing transformation and manifestation from God's Word.

...And it came to pass, that, as they went, they were cleansed. (Luke 17:14)

This passage is taken from the story of the ten lepers. Jesus healed them and told them to go and show themselves to the priests. They did not receive their full healing manifestation instantly; as they were on their way, they received their full healing manifestation (again, showing the process). Another example of the process would be the story of when Jesus cursed the fig tree. The fig tree did not die right then. It wasn't until the next day that the manifestation of what Jesus spoke the previous day came to pass.

It doesn't take God a long time to work a miracle. As you have seen many times in the Bible, healing can take place instantly. But many times God wants us to use the process of His Word. And again, just as taking physical medicine takes time, it also takes time for the spiritual process to work.

> *But they that wait upon the LORD shall renew their strength; they shall mount up with wings as eagles; they shall run, and not be weary; and they shall walk, and not faint. (Is 40:31)*

This passage has a double-fold meaning. First, it means to wait as in waiting on the manifestation (the process) to work. Sometimes we can get ahead of God by being impatient as in the story of Abraham with Isaac. Secondly, this passage refers to waiting upon the Lord as a waiter waits on customers in a restaurant. While you are waiting (in time) for the process of the manifestation, you also wait in service (through praying, reading, and confessing God's Word). And, in the process of time, God will renew your strength (your healing).

Chapter 2

Jesus, the Antidote for Our Sicknesses and Diseases

As we have discovered in Chapter 1, God is our Great Physician. His Word is our medicine. His medicine is the divine antidote for our sicknesses and diseases. But before we can learn about the antidote for our sicknesses and diseases, we need to go back to the beginning to find out how sickness and disease entered into the world and came upon man.

In the Beginning

In the beginning, God made Adam and Eve perfect creatures. They were made by God with incorruptible bodies that were never meant to be susceptible to old age, sickness, disease, nor any other malfunctions of the body. They were supposed to live forever in their god-like status. But then Satan came and tempted them, and they fell into sin.

God had previously told Adam that if they disobeyed Him and ate of the forbidden fruit, they would die. Well, Adam disobeyed, and they died. First, they died spiritually. Spiritual death is a separation from God's presence. They no longer had intimate, continual, daily fellowship with God. They were separated from God, His daily Word,

His power, and His presence. Secondly, their bodies began dying. The day they fell into sin, their bodies began decaying and growing old. Old age is a product of sin. As you look through the Bible, you never find an old angel. All angels are young. When we get our glorified bodies in heaven we will be forever young.

In addition to beginning to age the day they sinned, their bodies became susceptible to all of the sicknesses and diseases of the world. In their original state, their bodies were incapable of becoming sick. But after sin entered, so did their susceptibility to all kinds of sickness and disease.

Thirdly, because the wages of sin is death (referring to the second death of eternal hell), they were destined to spend their eternity in hell. When God declared that they would die if they ate from the forbidden tree and they disobeyed, they sealed their eternal fate. God's Word is irreversible, irrevocable, and unchangeable. There is nothing in the universe that can stop or change God's Word from coming to pass once it is spoken.

At this point, Satan thought he had won. Satan knew that God had to punish man's sin because of the Word He had spoken concerning sin. But he also knew that God loved man and did not want to punish man. Because of this dilemma, Satan thought that he would retain the keys to death, hell, and the grave forever and that man was destined to stay in this condition forever.

God Had a Plan

The problem with Satan's plan is that he could never outsmart God. God had a plan for mankind all along. Because God is all-knowing, He knew that mankind would fail and fall into sin. So in His infinite wisdom, God made a way to judge mankind's sins and uphold His Word to punish sin, and yet save and redeem man.

God's remedy to this divine dilemma was to select a supreme sacrifice that would be a substitute for mankind. God would pour out His wrath and judgment for the sin of all mankind upon this substitute and, thereby, keep His Word to punish sin, but yet save and redeem man.

To do this, God would need a perfect sacrificial lamb. It could not be an animal like the Old Testament animal sacrifices. They were mere animals, and none of them were perfect. Therefore, the blood of animals could only (temporarily) hide sin. It could not erase sin.

It could not be a mortal man because all of mankind inherited sin and the sin nature from Adam. Therefore, man's blood was imperfect and would not be accepted by God. The sacrifice had to be perfect and sinless. The only one in the universe that fit this qualification was God Himself in the person of Jesus Christ.

Jesus, the Sacrificial Lamb

Jesus is called the God-man. He is begotten of the Father and He is the image of the invisible God. He is one-hundred percent God, who is all-powerful and all-mighty. He is totally perfect, holy, and sinless. He was also flesh and blood, born of a woman, and one-hundred percent man. Yet, because His seed came from God and not from man, He did not inherit man's sinful blood and sinful nature.

His deity allowed Him to be the only perfect sacrifice that would be acceptable to God, and His humanity allowed Him to identify with man and represent mankind. All this made Him the perfect sacrifice.

> *The next day John seeth Jesus coming unto him, and saith, Behold the Lamb of God, which taketh away the sin of the world. (John 1:29)*

Jesus would become the Sacrificial Lamb of God. He would take man's place and suffer God's wrath and judgment in the place of man. All of God's wrath and judgment for disobedience and sin would be poured out and placed upon Jesus on the cross.

Christ suffered and died upon the cross to take away our sins. The story of Christ and the cross is not only in the New Testament, it is also seen throughout the Old Testament. A vivid picture of Christ and the cross can be seen in the following story of the Israelites in the wilderness.

The Pole and the Serpent

And the LORD said unto Moses, Make thee a fiery serpent, and set it upon a pole: and it shall come to pass, that every one that is bitten, when he looketh upon it, shall live. And Moses made a serpent of brass, and put it upon a pole, and it came to pass, that if a serpent had bitten any man, when he beheld the serpent of brass, he lived. (Num 21:8-9)

In the above passage, while in the wilderness, the children of Israel once again angered God with their sin and rebellion. Because of this, God sent poisonous snakes upon them. Many people died from the poisonous bite of the snakes. After the children of Israel realized that this happened because of their sin and rebellion, they cried out to God and repented.

God accepted their repentance and gave Moses instructions on what to do about the snake bites. He told Moses to make a brass serpent on a pole. He gave instructions to Moses that if anyone was bitten by the serpents, to look upon the brass serpent on the pole, and they would live and not die.

A Picture of the Cross

All of this was a picture and symbolism of God's plan of redemption for us. It was a picture of Christ on the cross. The serpents represented sin. It was because of the Israelites sin that God sent the serpents. Those that died represent what happens to people who die in their sin (without Christ) — referring to the second death of eternal hell. Brass represents God's judgment for sin. The pole represented the cross.

So when you put it all together, it was a picture of God's judgment upon mankind through Jesus Christ on the cross. The serpent on the pole was a picture of Jesus on the cross because He took our sins and bore them upon His own body on the cross, thereby, becoming sin for us.

For he hath made him to be sin for us, who knew no sin; that we might be made the righteousness of God in him. (2 Co 5:21)

Looking unto Jesus

Again, the Israelites were instructed to look at the serpent on the pole if they were bitten. After looking at the serpent on the pole, they would live and not die. This illustration had a two-fold meaning. As we have discovered, first, it means that if we look unto Jesus for our salvation and receive Him, we will not die the eternal death of hell. We will live eternally with God.

Secondly, if they were bitten, they were physically healed and lived when they looked unto the serpent on the pole. Since we now know the serpent on the pole is a picture of Jesus and the cross, this means that we can also be physically healed when we are bitten with sickness and disease as we look to Jesus upon the cross.

Looking at the picture of Jesus and the cross became their antidote. Jesus is also our antidote today for sickness and disease. Just as they were able to look at the symbol of Jesus upon the cross and were healed, we can much more abundantly receive our healing when we look to the actual true cross. The question is: Just how do we look to Jesus? The answer to that question lies in you knowing who Jesus is.

> *In the beginning was the Word, and the Word was with God, and the Word was God.... And the Word was made flesh, and dwelt among us, (and we beheld his glory, the glory as of the only begotten of the Father,) full of grace and truth. (John 1:1-3, 14)*

The above passage plainly shows us that Jesus is the Word of God. So, the first way that we look to Jesus is to keep our eyes on the Word.

"Let them not depart from thine eyes...."

In Chapter 1, we discovered that God's instructions for us concerning His medicine is to *"Let His Word not depart from our eyes."* We are to keep our eyes continuously focused on Jesus (The Word of God). This means that whatever you are going through, find the Word that deals with your need and keep it before your eyes.

This passage does not mean that you keep the Bible in front of your face 24 hours a day. What it means is that you are to keep your mind focused on the Word of God on a continuous basis. It means the same as in 1 Thes 5:17 where the Bible tells us to *pray without ceasing*.

This refers to a continual, steadfast, and focused attitude on the Word of God. It means that when you get up in the morning you look to Jesus; throughout your workday take time to look to Jesus; when you get home from work take a moment to look to Jesus; and before you go to bed, take a moment to look to Jesus. It also means to meditate and keep your mind on Jesus.

As we discovered in Chapter 1, *"incline"* means to "lean forward." In other words, it means that we pay close attention with a steadfast focus on Jesus (who is the Word).

Looking unto Jesus does not mean that you get regimental like the Muslims and pray three times a day at a specific time. It means that you develop a lifestyle and an attitude of constantly looking at the Word when you have opportunities.

If you need healing, there are 160 scriptures and confessions in our last chapter that will help aid and assist you. Develop a pattern and lifestyle of looking unto Jesus through these scriptures and confessions each day, several times a day. Eventually, it will become second nature so that when you have time, you will be drawn to look to Jesus.

Looking unto the Word is not only something we do with our eyes. We also look to the Word by listening to and receiving His Word in our hearts. Even when you listen to the Word being preached, you are looking to the Word. And as you continue to keep your eyes focused upon the cross, you will receive your healing.

In our next chapter, we will look at the second way we look to Jesus and receive our healing: by looking unto His sufferings.

Chapter 3

Healing Through His Sufferings

In our previous chapter we discovered that the children of Israel received their healing while in the wilderness when they looked unto the picture of Jesus and the cross. Therefore, we can also look to Jesus and receive our healing. We found that the first way we look to Jesus is to look at and focus on Him as the Word of God. In this chapter, we want to look at another way in which we can look to Jesus and receive our healing — which is to look unto His sufferings.

Seeing His Sufferings

When it comes to someone suffering, we usually like to avoid seeing it. Whether it's soldiers suffering from an injury, pain, and other hardships of war, starving children suffering and dying of malnutrition, or someone dying of a debilitating disease, we all prefer to avoid seeing the actual suffering as much as we can.

But in the case of the sufferings of Jesus and the cross, seeing His sufferings is a good thing for us. This is why God did not want us to avoid seeing His sufferings. In fact, God chronicled every single detail of the sufferings of Christ in His Word for us to see and visualize. It's in properly seeing, visualizing, and reflecting upon His sufferings that we are able to reap the benefits, blessings, and the healing of God.

The occasion that we most often remember and reflect upon His sufferings is when we partake in Holy Communion. Through partaking in Holy Communion, many people have been healed of cancer, diabetes, arthritis, heart disease and a host of other illnesses and diseases. In this chapter we want to look at how seeing and reflecting upon the sufferings of Christ in Holy Communion can unlock the door to our divine healing.

Missing the Focus

Most of us are used to taking Holy Communion in our churches and going through all the rituals and formalities. All these things are good. And with the proper heart towards the Lord's Supper, they show honor and reverence to our Lord. However, even though all these things may make the Holy Communion service look and feel like we are doing something sacred and holy before God, these things are not the focus of Holy Communion.

> *And when he had given thanks, he brake it, and said, Take, eat: this is my body, which is broken for you: this do in remembrance of me. After the same manner also he took the cup, when he had supped, saying, This cup is the new testament in my blood: this do ye, as oft as ye drink it, in remembrance of me. (1 Co 11:24-25)*

In the above passage, Jesus was serving Communion for the first time to His disciples. He did not give any instructions on how to dress, what to use, what to say, or how to perform the ceremony. His instructions to them was the same as it is to us today: As often as we partake in Holy Communion, to do so, *"In Remembrance of Him."* The focus of Jesus' instructions was not in the ceremony. It was in the *"remembrance"* of Him. The remembrance He is referring to is the remembrance of His sufferings on our behalf.

I have seen ministers and priests perform Holy Communion in services that looked good but never even mention anything about the sufferings of Christ. Remembering the sufferings of Christ was Jesus' primary instructions. You have not truly partaken in Holy Communion if you have not taken time to remember Him in His sufferings.

Why would Jesus put the emphasis in Holy Communion on remembering His sufferings? It's because remembering and reflecting upon the sufferings of Christ during Holy Communion releases the power of God to be healed and receive our blessings. Let me say that again: *REMEMBERING AND REFLECTING UPON THE SUFFERINGS OF CHRIST DURING HOLY COMMUNION RELEASES THE POWER OF GOD TO BE HEALED AND RECEIVE GOD'S BLESSINGS.*

There is power for us to be healed when we remember His sufferings. Let's look at a very familiar passage of scripture regarding our healing as it relates to His sufferings.

By His Stripes and Sufferings We Are Healed

He is despised and rejected of men; a man of sorrows, and acquainted with grief: and we hid as it were our faces from him; he was despised, and we esteemed him not. Surely he hath borne our griefs, and carried our sorrows: yet we did esteem him stricken, smitten of God, and afflicted. But he was wounded for our transgressions, he was bruised for our iniquities: the chastisement of our peace was upon him; and with his stripes we are healed. (Is 53:3-5)

When we quote this scripture pertaining to our healing, most people only quote the last six words (*...and with his stripes we are healed*). But the power of the last six words regarding our healing also lies in us understanding and properly remembering and reflecting on His sufferings in the whole passage. Let us look further into this passage as it relates His sufferings to our salvation, healing, deliverance, and blessings.

He Was Despised and Rejected for Us...

He was not only despised and rejected by the Pharisees and others who hated Him, He had to also endure being despised and rejected by His own people. Many of them were people who He had fed, performed miracles, showed kindness, and healed. He had to even endure being rejected by His own disciples. He was despised and rejected of men so that we would never have to be despised and rejected by God because of our sins.

Not only was he rejected of men, He had to also endure being rejected by God. In an earlier chapter, we said that spiritual death is a separation from God. Jesus also endured a spiritual death for us. When Jesus was upon the cross, He cried out to the Father, *"My God, My God, why have You forsaken Me?"* At that moment while He was upon the cross, God placed all the sin and iniquity for all of mankind upon Jesus. Because God is holy and cannot be connected with sin in any manner, He had to separate Himself from His only loving Son, Jesus Christ, for hours while he hung on the cross.

This was key for us because Jesus suffered being separated from God so that we would never have to be separated from Him either in this life, or for all eternity.

He Was Falsely Accused...

Further down in this passage in Verse 8, it says that He was taken from prison to the judgment hall. The purpose of them taking Him to the judgment hall was to accuse Him. Since they couldn't find any sin, fault, or wrongdoing in Him, they falsely accused him. This was on our behalf. He carried all of our guilt, condemnation, shame, and accusations made by satan, every demonic spirit, and every person satan uses to attack us. Because he carried all of them for us, satan cannot stand against us while on earth or in judgment and accuse us of any sin, transgression, iniquity, or wrongdoing. This is because Jesus carried them all for us upon His own body and nailed them to the cross. For those who do not accept Christ, satan will be their prosecutor accusing them of all the sins they have committed during their lifetime. But for those of us who accept and receive Christ, satan will not be able to accuse us of even one sin because Jesus took all of the accusations against us and bore them on His own body on the cross. Praise God!

He Was Wounded and Bruised for Us...

But he was wounded for our transgressions, he was bruised for our iniquities: the chastisement of our peace was upon him; and with his stripes we are healed. (Is 53:3-5)

The wounds and bruises He took were to pay the penalty for all of our sins. The wounds from the nails in His hands and feet were for every one of our sins, iniquities, transgressions, and disobediences. Not only did they pay for the ones we did in the past, they also paid for the ones in our present and in our future. His wounds and bruises paid the full and complete price for the wages of our sins so that we can be healed and set free.

The Chastisement of Our Peace Was upon Him...

At Christmas time, we often see the phrase: *"Peace on earth, good will towards men."* Many people relate that to a time when there will be peace on earth in terms of war and troubles. But there has always been war and troubles in the earth, and there will always be war and troubles until God takes us to glory.

When God said, *"Peace on earth,"* He was not referring to war and troubles. He was referring to peace between God and man. When Adam sinned, it caused a war between us (our rebellious flesh and nature) and God. This war lasted from Adam's sin until the sacrifice of Jesus. During this time, there was no peace in man's spirit or soul with God. Neither was their any intimate fellowship between God and man. It was war and separation. *The chastisement of our peace* represents the sufferings and torture Jesus endured for us to give us peace in our spirit and soul with God. His sacrifice did away with sin, thereby, opening peace relations with God and man. His chastisement upon the cross caused the veil in the temple to be torn (representing the separation between God and man), allowing us to be able to enter into God's presence and receive His peaceful fellowship and communion once again.

With His Stripes We Are Healed...

The reason that we can declare that we are healed by His stripes is because His stripes represent all the sufferings He endured to pay the penalty for our sins. Sickness and disease upon mankind are penalties for man's sins and disobedience. But Jesus suffered and died to pay the penalty for our sins — thereby releasing us from having to pay the penalty of sickness and disease. It's like Jesus erased our criminal (sinful) record with God, releasing us from having to pay the penalty ourselves.

Jesus' sufferings took away the accusations and guilt of our sins, which also took away the need for the penalty of sickness and disease. Since there is now no sin (Because Christ took away our sins), there should also not be a penalty for sickness and disease. And, if sickness and disease is upon you, then it is there unlawfully.

It would be like putting a person in jail that is completely innocent with no accusation, proof, or evidence against them. Because they are innocent and there is no guilt or accusation against them, they can demand their release (if they know their rights according to the law). And by the rights they have in the law, they must be released. Likewise, since Christ has paid the penalty for our sins, we can also decree, declare, and demand that we be released from the bondage of sickness and disease, provided that we also know our rights and privileges according God's Word.

Once we know our rights and demand our release, Satan has to release us and let us go (from sickness and disease). We can demand this because Jesus paid the price— leaving us sin-free, guilt-free, and penalty-free. So when you declare that you are healed by the stripes of Jesus Christ, remember, His stripes (and other sufferings) paid the penalty, which allows us to be set free and receive our healing and deliverance.

More than 39 Stripes

I want to clear up something that is often misquoted concerning this passage. When people say that Jesus took 39 stripes on His back for us, this is incorrect. When they say that Jesus took 39 stripes, they are mis-referencing Paul's account of the 39 stripes he received for preaching about Jesus (2 Cor 11:24).

Jewish law (Deut 25:1-3) limited the amount of lashes a person could receive for breaking the law or committing a crime to 40 stripes. Since the Jews were legalistic and did not want to break the law, they stopped at 39 stripes just in case they miscounted.

But in the case of Jesus, even though they beat, spat on Him, pulled His beard, and committed other abuses during His arrest and (false) trial, He did not receive any stripes by the Jews. They despised Him so much that even though they could have given Him 39 stripes, they wanted death instead.

Pilate's Decision

Under Roman law, the Jews were not allowed to put anyone to death. This is why they turned Him over to Pilate to have Him crucified. Pilate really didn't want to crucify Jesus because He knew that He was innocent and that the Pharisees only persecuted Jesus out of envy, jealousy, and fear of losing their positions. He thought that if he had Jesus severely scourged, that it would appease their hatred for Jesus and desire for His death, and he would be able to let Jesus go. But when the Pharisees basically said that they would appeal to Caesar and would say that Pilate was allowing another person to be called king (other than Caesar), Pilate yielded to their request.

At this point, Pilate saw his position being threatened and chose to crucify Jesus. He did this even though he knew Jesus was innocent because he didn't want to risk jeopardizing his position as governor.

Jesus' Scourging

Now, let us go back to Pilate granting permission to have Jesus scourged. Again, the Jews could only give 39 stripes. However, the Romans did not have any such restriction on how many stripes they could give or even what type of stripes they could administer. They would often beat the person until either they themselves became tired or to within an inch of the person's death (so that they could still crucify the person).

They used an assortment of whips. These whips had an array of imbedded articles in them that would mutilate the body and immensely elevate the level of torture and pain. These whips were attached with pieces of bone, wood, metal, and even hooks that would tear, gouge, and viciously rip out pieces and chunks of flesh.

The following is a passage that is taken from the book of

Isaiah that describes in scripture how Jesus looked after His scourging.

> ...His [Jesus] appearance was so disfigured beyond that of any human being; and His form [was] marred beyond human likeness. (Is 52:15) NIV

This passage correctly describes how Jesus looked after His severe scourging. This description goes far beyond someone who was only given 39 stripes with a nice clean leather strap. Instead, it describes someone who had undergone many, countless whips of torture, pain, agony, and mutilation.

I believe that God used Mel Gipson to produce *"the Passion of the Christ"* to give us a close visualization of how severely they scourged and beat Jesus. Even though the movie showed quite a bit, I don't even believe that this movie was a correct depiction of how many stripes He received, the severity of His beating, and the mutilation of His body.

So the next time you declare that you are healed by the stripes of Jesus Christ, remember the true severity of what He undertook and painfully, agonizingly endured so that we could be healed.

His Stripes Covers so much More

The Bible often refers to the stripes of Jesus Christ for our healing, and the cross for our salvation and redemption. But when the Bible refers to the cross or the stripes Jesus endured for us, it is also referencing all the wounds, bruises, pain, and agony Jesus suffered on our behalf. This covers everything from the time they arrested Him in the Garden of Gethsemane until He hung His head and died on the cross.

The following is a list of "some" of the sufferings Jesus had to endure on our behalf. When you partake in Holy Communion, refer to this list from time to time to remember and reflect upon what Jesus had to endure for our redemption, salvation, deliverance, and our healing:

A List of Some of the Sufferings Jesus Endured:

- They beat Him when they arrested Him and took Him to the judgment hall.
- They falsely accused Him.
- He was imprisoned for crimes that He was innocent of.
- He was rejected and abandoned the night He was arrested.
- He was further rejected, denied, and abandoned by His own disciples.
- The Romans tied Him and whipped Him with many stripes.
- They whipped Him with an assortment of tortuous whips.
- They mashed a crown of thorns into His scalp.
- He was sentenced to death as an innocent man.
- They gave Him more stripes while making Him carry His own heavy cross.
- He collapsed after His body was beaten and worn to complete exhaustion while carrying His cross.
- They nailed His hands and feet to the cross and hung Him up.
- They associated Him with and hung Him between two common thieves.
- He suffered on the cross in great agony and pain for several hours.
- He had the weight of the sins, iniquities, and transgressions of the world placed upon Him.
- He had the weight of all of our sicknesses, diseases, and afflictions placed on Him.
- He had to be separated from the Father for several hours while carrying our sins and iniquities.
- He was ridiculed and scoffed by many as He hung on the cross.
- He hung His head and died.
- They pierced Him in His side.

As you can see, in addition to the horrific mutilation that Jesus endured by the Romans during His scouring, He suffered so much more. In the future, when you make a reference to the stripes of Jesus Christ regarding your healing or the sufferings of the cross to redeem us, know that it entails so much more.

The Purpose of the Cross

Jesus Christ is the true, perfect sacrificial Lamb of God. We know that He had to come and shed His perfect, sinless blood for us for the forgiveness of our sins. The blood of the Old Testament animals could only hide and cover man's sins, not erase them. The blood of animals only covered and hid man's sins for one year. This was done year after year until Jesus came and shed His blood for us.

The blood of Jesus Christ was perfect and sinless. His blood not only covered our sins, but completely erased them forever. Praise God for Jesus Christ, by whose blood we are forgiven and justified by God through grace, through faith in Christ and in His blood.

The question then remains, "what was the purpose for the cross?" If the only thing that was required by God for our sin to be forgiven was the blood of Jesus to be shed and placed on the mercy seat of heaven, why did Jesus have to also suffer on the cross? Why couldn't God have used the blood from the many stripes that tore into His back causing blood to be shed, or the blood from the crown of thorns that was mashed into His scalp, or any other sufferings He endured that shed His blood? To answer this question we have to find out what the cross represents.

> *And if a man have committed a sin worthy of death, and he be to be put to death, and thou hang him on a tree: ...(for <u>he that is hanged is accursed</u> of God;).... Deu 21:22-23*
>
> *Christ hath redeemed us from the curse of the law, being made a curse for us: for it is written, <u>Cursed is every one that hangeth on a tree</u>: Gal 3:13*

According to scripture, to hang on a tree was considered a curse by God. The reason why Jesus had to be hung on a tree (the cross) was because the cross represented our curse. When man sinned and rebelled against God, it brought the curse of disobedience against man. Remember, the wages of sin is death. The spirit of death brought sickness and disease as a curse. Man was never meant to have sickness and disease. They were a byproduct of the curse of disobedience. The curse of disobedience also included sin, shame, condemnation, the penalty of hell, and many other things.

Again, it would have been enough for Jesus to shed His blood and die for us. But even though His bloodshed would have covered our sins, it would not have completely removed the curse of disobedience that was upon mankind, and we still would have been openly susceptible to the curse of sickness and disease and many other things because of the curse of disobedience.

The tree (cross) represents the curse. Jesus became the curse for us by not only shedding His blood, but by also hanging (being crucified) on the tree (the cross). Therefore, His death on the cross released us from all the penalties of the curse—including sickness and diseases associated with the curse.

When Jesus said, "It is finished," He was saying that everything had been paid, including the payment for the curse of disobedience in which sickness and disease is included. Therefore, since Christ took and became the curse for us on the cross, the curse against us has been completely paid, eradicated, finished, and removed.

With this understanding, we can now come boldly before the throne of grace and declare with power and authority that we are healed from all sickness and diseases because of the payment and covering of the blood of Jesus Christ, and the removal of every curse, by the sufferings of Jesus Christ on the cross for us.

Chapter 4

A Picture of Our Healing in the Passover

The picture of God's healing grace is clearly seen in the stripes He endured and the suffering of the cross. It is also seen in the parallel picture of the cross with the Passover. Let's take another look at God's divine plan of healing for us in the Passover.

> *He brought them forth also with silver and gold: and there was not one feeble person among their tribes. (Ps 105:37)*

This passage tells us that when they came out of Egypt, there was not one sick person in their midst. This passage refers to the morning after the Passover. There were over two million Jews that came out of Egypt, and every one of them who had any kind of sickness, disease, or illness was healed. Why did this massive healing take place? It was because of their obedience to God's instructions the night before they came out of Egypt.

God had instructed them to kill a lamb and place the blood of the lamb on the doorposts of their houses. During the night, the death angel came and killed the firstborn of all those who did not have the blood on their doorposts. The Lamb represents Jesus Christ. The doorposts represent the cross.

> *And they shall eat the flesh [of the Passover Lamb] in that night, roast with fire, and unleavened bread; and with bitter herbs they shall eat it. (Exo 12:8)*

In the above passage, God instructed them to roast the Passover lamb with fire and eat it with bitter herbs. Placing the blood on their doorposts, and eating the body of the Passover lamb (representing eating the body of Jesus) healed their bodies.

Feeding on the Lamb

> *Then Jesus said unto them, Verily, verily, I say unto you, Except ye eat the flesh of the Son of man, and drink his blood, ye have no life in you. (John 6:53)*

This passage is a New Testament (spiritual) version and parallel of the same (physical) passage above in Exodus. When Jesus spoke this passage in the book of John, many left Him because they thought He was speaking of some type of cannibalism. They did not understand that this passage was not to be taken literally but rather spiritually. They obeyed the Old Testament law and ate the physical Passover lamb, but they did not understand that Jesus was the spiritual Passover Lamb whom they were now supposed to eat spiritually.

Eating to Survive

Everything in this world feeds on something. Plants take the energy from sunlight and convert it to food. Animals eat plants (and other animals). As humans, we eat plants (and animals) as food, and our bodies convert the food to energy which enables us to live.

If you cut off the food source of any plant or animal, then they will die. Jesus applies this same principle when He says that unless we eat of His flesh and drink of His blood, we have no life in us. Jesus is simply saying that we need to eat of Him to survive.

God designed the physical realm so that everything in the earth exists from the life of the "sun." The Bible clearly tells us that Jesus is the source of all life. So just as the "sun" is the source of all life physically, the "Son"—Jesus Christ, is the source of all life spiritually as well as physically. So when Jesus refers to us eating His flesh, He is referring to us feeding off of Him spiritually. We feed off of Him by feeding off His Word, His Spirit, His virtue, and His anointing. We also feed off of Him when we meditate on Him, when we worship Him, when we hear His Word, and when we pray. All of these (and others) are different types of ways that we eat the body of Christ.

Eating the Lamb Raw

Again, when they ate of the Passover lamb, they were instructed to roast the lamb with fire and eat it with bitter herbs. The fire and bitter herbs represented all the sufferings Jesus had to go through in order to redeem us. Jesus was roasted, cooked, and prepared by the fire of God's affliction and judgment so that we can now eat of Him.

Eating the lamb raw represents several things. First, it represents us trying to obtain God's salvation, righteousness, grace, healing, and His blessings without coming through Christ. When we attempt to come to God or even try to pray without coming through Christ, we are attempting to eat the lamb raw.

Eating the lamb raw is to also try to obtain God's goodness, healing, and blessings by trying to do so through the law. In other words, through our own self-righteousness.

This was the problem that the rich young ruler had. Some people think they can obtain God's blessings through their (personal interpretation of) obedience to the law. None of us can obtain righteousness through the law because none of us can obey the whole, full law. Because if you offend one single thing in the law, you offend the whole law. And, the truth is that no matter how good we think we are, *all of us have sinned and come short of God's glory.*

Eating the lamb raw is to also try to earn our way to God's salvation, healing, and blessings by our good deeds and works. Without God's proper preparation of the Lamb, none of our works or deeds is acceptable by God. For God's Word has declared that *all of our good works and righteousness are like filthy rags before the Lord.* None of them makes us worthy of receiving God's salvation, healing, or blessings.

Are We Animals or Humans?

As humans, God made us different from animals. Animals were made to be able to eat meat raw. But God made us as humans to eat meat after it has been cooked and prepared. In the Bible, God refers to different people as animals, as it relates to the eating habits of animals. If we, as humans, attempt to eat the Lamb of God raw, then we too can be considered as animals by our eating habits.

Man had to wait for thousands of years until the appointed time had come for God to cook, prepare, and roast the Lamb of God for us. Now that He has been properly cooked and prepared by God for us, God wants us to now come and freely feed and feast off Him. And, as we feed off Him, we can be nourished, healed, and live.

Eating with Grace

The only proper way for us to eat of the Lamb is to receive it with grace. This is to know that there is nothing we can do to earn our salvation, healing, or blessings. It was all of God's love, His mercy, His goodness, and His sacrifice. That's why He deserves "ALL" of the worship, adoration, thanksgiving, and praise.

Discerning the Lord's Body

For he that eateth and drinketh unworthily, eateth and drinketh damnation to himself, not discerning the Lord's body. For this cause many are weak and sickly among you, and many sleep. (1 Co 11:29-30)

This passage is showing us something very important concerning Communion. It is saying that if anyone eats and drinks the Lord's Supper in an unworthy manner by failing to discern the body of the Lord, it can cause illness, sickness, and even premature death. In the same manner, we can also conclude that if we eat of the Lord's Supper and properly discern and understand the Lord's body, it will instead bring us wholeness, healing, and health. Let me say that again, *"PROPERLY PARTAKING AND DISCERNING OF THE LORD'S BODY CAN BRING WHOLENESS, HEALING, AND HEALTH TO YOUR BODY."*

To properly discern the Lord's body is to give reverence, respect, and honor to God for the body and blood of Jesus Christ that you are about to eat and drink.

Once you ask God to bless it as the blood and body of our Lord, it is no longer crackers and juice (or whatever you are using). To God, at that point, you are actually eating and drinking the broken and prepared body and blood of Jesus Christ. To disrespect and dishonor it at that point is to disrespect and dishonor the Lord.

Properly discerning the Lord's body is to also understand what you are doing and not take it lightly. This is why I suggest teaching your children at a young age about Holy Communion and what it truly represents. If not, to them, they will see it only as a snack. We also dishonor the Lord's body when we do not take the time to remember and reflect upon His supreme sacrifice and the sufferings He endured for us. Again, Jesus instructed us to *(do this)* partake in Holy Communion in remembrance of Him and the sufferings of His sacrificial death. So, when we partake in Holy Communion with a distracted mind, or we do not properly remember His sacrificial death, we are eating the Lamb raw. And, finally, we dishonor Him when we don't take a moment to give Him praise and thanksgiving for what He has done.

Closing:

The Israelites were *"all"* healed when they came out of Egypt because they obeyed the Word of the Lord and ate of the Passover lamb. That was not just a one-time event for the Israelites. Remember, God is the same yesterday, today, and forever. What He did for them thousands of years ago, He is still doing for us today. If they were healed by eating of what was only a picture of the real New Testament Passover Lamb, how much more can we receive our healing when we eat of the true Passover Lamb, Jesus Christ.

We have also discovered that we can eat of the Passover Lamb, Jesus Christ, in two ways: First, we eat of Him when we eat of Him as the Word of God. Secondly, we eat of Him when we eat His broken body and drink His blood in Holy Communion.

Just as the Israelites ate their way to healing and health, we can also eat our way to health when we eat of the Lamb of God. Jesus Christ, the true Passover Lamb, has been prepared and roasted on the cross as a meal for us by God. God now invites us to come and eat of Him through both His Word and through Holy Communion. As we eat of Him, we can and will be blessed, delivered, and healed.

Chapter 5

Instructions for Taking Holy Communion

Now that you have been given information about Holy Communion, what it represents, what it does, and how it pertains to your healing, you should want to begin taking Holy Communion at home. The following are instructions that will guide you step-by-step in taking communion at home.

After these instructions, there are additional answers to some of the questions that you may have pertaining to taking personal Holy Communion.

1. Give God Thanks and Ask for His Blessings
<u>Mark 14:23</u> *And when he had given thanks, he gave it to them…*
Luke 24:30 *…He… blessed it, and brake, and gave to them.*

Prayer: Father, I thank You for Your great and awesome love for us. For You so loved us that You gave Your only Son, Jesus Christ, whose body was broken and whose blood was poured out for us, in order to redeem and cleanse us. I give You thanksgiving, glory, honor, and praise for Your great love and Your supreme sacrifice. I ask that You would now supernaturally bless this bread and this juice (or whatever you are using) as the body and blood of our Lord, Jesus Christ, as I prepare to partake in the Lord's Supper.

2. Examine Yourself
1 Co 11:28 But let a man examine himself,
and so let him eat of that bread, and drink of that cup.

PRAYER: Father, I ask by Your grace and mercy that You would forgive me of all of my sins, iniquities, and transgressions. Forgive me for those that I have done knowingly, as well as those I have done unknowingly. I ask that You would cover me with Your precious blood so that I may be counted worthy to partake of and receive Your body and Your blood.

* At this time examine your heart before the Lord. Repent of any known sin, malice, strife, and unforgiveness in your heart and life. Once you have done this (from your heart), you have now properly examined yourself, and you are now ready to partake of the Lord's Supper.

3. Remembrance of His Broken Body:
1 Co 11:24 …Take, eat: this is my body, which is broken for you:
<u>*this do in remembrance of me.*</u>

PRAYER: Lord Jesus, You said that as often as we eat this bread, that we should do so in remembrance of You. Lord, I want to thank You for the sufferings that You endured on my behalf. I thank You that they: *(name several things that they did to the Lord's body. Use page 36 as a reference).* And because You endured the stripes and sufferings for me, my body *(or whatever you are believing to be restored)* is healed, restored, and made whole.

Because of Christ, I claim my total and complete healing from the crown of my head to the soles of my feet. Every cell, every organ, every function of my body is healed, restored, and renewed. In Jesus Name, I thank You.

Note: If you are taking Communion for something else other than physical healing, replace the last paragraph with claiming your victory in that particular area.

* {Now go ahead and eat of His body}.

4. Remembrance of His Shed Blood

1 Co 11:25 …he took the cup…saying, This cup is the new testament in my blood: this do ye, as oft as ye drink it, in remembrance of me.

Prayer: Lord, in addition to the sufferings of Your body, You also shed your blood for us. I thank You for *(name several things they did in shedding His blood).* Through Your blood, You became the sacrificial Lamb of God for us. My sin-free, disease-free, poverty-free life is in Your blood. And Your shed blood has removed every sin from my life. Through Your blood, I am forgiven of all my sins—past, present and future—and I am made completely righteous. Today, I celebrate and partake of the inheritance of Your righteousness: which is preservation, healing, wholeness and provisions. By the righteousness of Your blood, I claim my victory *(name the area that you are claiming).*

* {Now go ahead and drink of His blood}.

5. Closing Prayer

Now Lord, as Jesus hung on the cross before He died, He declared that the work He came to accomplish was finished. I, therefore, declare by the power of the cross and the blood of Jesus Christ that the healing and deliverance for *(your body, relationships, finances, bondages, addictions, or whatever you are believing for)* is also finished, accomplished, and completed. I believe and receive it in the name of our Lord, Jesus Christ.

6. Closing Scripture

Jesus' sacrifice on the cross gave us benefits that we should claim according to His Word. Many of them can be found in this passage. I recommend closing with this passage:

Prayer: *(Ps 103:1-5)* Bless the LORD, O my soul: and all that is within me, bless His holy name. Bless the LORD, O my soul, and forget not all His benefits: Who forgives all my iniquities; <u>who heals all my sickness and diseases</u>; who redeems my life from every destruction and attack of the enemy; who crowns me with loving-kindness and tender mercies; who blesses my life with good things; *and <u>who renews my life, health, and strength</u> like the eagle's.*

To God be all the glory and praise. In the name of our Lord, Jesus Christ. AMEN.

Frequently Asked Questions About Home Communion

I believe the teaching on Holy Communion has answered most questions you may have had. However, there are a few questions I would like to answer that are frequently asked regarding Holy Communion at home. They are as follows:

1. Does Holy Communion Have to Be Done at Church?

No. Acts 2:46 tells us that they took Holy Communion in the temple, and they also had it in their homes. Although Holy Communion can be partaken in a church gathering, it can also be partaken in a small family setting with your family, friends, or in a personal, intimate fellowship with just you and the Lord.

2. Who Is Authorized to Serve Holy Communion?

At church, the pastor or priest, elder, minister, or deacon usually leads Communion. However, when Jesus taught it to His disciples, they represented us. We are Jesus' disciples. In addition, 1 Peter 2:9 declares that as born-again Christians, we are God's royal priesthood. This also authorizes you to perform Holy Communion at home.

3. How Often Should We Partake of Holy Communion at Home?

Jesus did not give any specific instructions as to the frequency that we should partake in Holy Communion. However, He did say, "as often as you choose." Jesus left it up to us as to the frequency. I believe that is because it will depend on what you are going through. On average, I believe that we should partake in home Communion at minimum once a week. But if you are going though a severe storm or serious attack in your life, I believe that you should partake each and every day. Some choose to partake several times a day when they are under serious attack.

4. Is Home Holy Communion Only for Physical Healing?

No. The stripes of Jesus Christ provided healing and wholeness for every part of your life. You can receive wholeness in any area of your life—spiritually, physically, or financially. You can also claim wholeness and healing by the stripes of Jesus Christ in your marriage, children's lives, or any other area of concern in your life.

5. Do We Repeat the Communion Instructions Verbatim?

No. They are only guidelines. However, I think that the guidelines are scriptural and coincide with Jesus' instructions to us for Holy Communion. The main focus is to ask God to bless whatever you are using as the body and blood of Jesus Christ. It is to also reflect upon the sufferings He endured on our behalf, and give Him thanksgiving and praise for His love and sacrifice for us.

6. What Kind of Bread or Juice Should We Use?

The type of bread or juice you use is not as important as what they represent. For bread, you can use any bread by-product such as bread of any kind or crackers. For the juice, you can use any liquid such as any juice, soda, Kool-Aid, or any liquid. But once you ask God to bless and sanctify them (as far as God sees them), they become the actual broken body and blood of Jesus Christ no matter what you physically use.

For those who would like to hear a message on Holy Communion, I have a CD message that may give you more understanding. To request yours, go to:
www.prayerwarfare.com

―――― Chapter 6 ――――

Is Healing Just for the Righteous?

The eyes of the LORD are upon the righteous and his ears are open unto their cry. (Ps 34:15)

As we read the Bible, we see many scriptures like the one above that references God's healing and blessings being reserved for the righteous. The word *"righteous"* can be found 238 times in the Bible. Without proper knowledge and understanding about our righteousness in Christ, these types of scriptures may cause some people to believe that God's divine healing (and other blessings) are only for the righteous. In fact, Romans 3:23 tells us that *all of us have sinned and come short of God's glory*.

The devil knows how to use our past failures and mistakes to condemn us with the very Word of God we are using to receive our healing. He is quick to remind us that the promises of God's Word (that we are attempting to quote) are for the righteous, while at the same time bringing up a laundry list to us of our past sins and transgressions. So if the blessings of God are reserved for the righteous, where does that leave us? Don't worry. God has not abandoned us. He has made a way for us to receive our healing in spite of our sins and shortcomings. Let's look at the following story with Hezekiah to see more about this subject.

Hezekiah's Healing

In those days was Hezekiah sick unto death. And the prophet Isaiah... said unto him, Thus saith the LORD, Set thine house in order; for thou shalt die, and not live. Then he turned his face to the wall, and prayed unto the LORD, saying, I beseech thee, O LORD, remember now how I have walked before thee in truth and with a perfect heart, and have done that which is good in thy sight... And it came to pass, afore Isaiah was gone out into the middle court, that the word of the LORD came to him, saying, Turn again, and tell Hezekiah the captain of my people, Thus saith the LORD, the God of David thy father, I have heard thy prayer, I have seen thy tears: behold, I will heal thee... And I will add unto thy days fifteen years... (2Ki 20:1-6)

This story of Hezekiah's healing is very familiar to most Christians. Isaiah, the prophet, had been sent by God to give Hezekiah a message to get his affairs in order because his (Hezekiah's) death was near. Hezekiah immediately turned his face to the wall and began crying out to God. God mercifully heard his prayer, and before Isaiah could leave the court area, God gave Isaiah another Word and told him to go back and tell Hezekiah that he was going to heal him and add 15 years to his life.

This is a wonderful and encouraging story regarding our healing, until you look at what Hezekiah said to the Lord before the Lord granted his healing. When Hezekiah turned his face to the wall, he began to pray this prayer: *"remember now how I have walked before thee in truth and with a perfect heart, and have done that which is good in thy sight..."* In this prayer Hezekiah almost sounds conceited. He reminded the Lord of his own righteousness, good deeds, and merits, and God heard him, answered his prayer and healed him. Under the old covenant, this was a way to approach God, because healing and blessings (as well as curses) were sent by God on the basis of a person's obedience or disobedience.

The problem with the old covenant is that not many of us could boast to God (who is the God of all righteousness) about any of our good works or deeds. Romans 3:12 tells us that *there is no one that does good* (in the sight of God), *not even one person.* So if our healing were based upon us being able to remind God of our righteousness, most of us would have to settle for being sick.

But thanks be to God that we live under a much better covenant than Hezekiah lived under. Under the new covenant, our healing and blessings are not based upon our righteousness, but rather on Christ's righteousness. When we come to God for our healing, we do not do like Hezekiah did and remind God of our righteousness (because we do not have any in His sight). We remind God of Christ's righteousness. Because we are covered by the blood of Jesus Christ, we are also covered by His righteousness. And, when God looks at us, He sees us as the righteous in Christ.

So, you have a right to do like Hezekiah and ask for your healing based on righteousness. But it must be based upon the righteousness you have in Christ. And it's because of Christ's righteousness that God grants our healing.

The Great Exchange

For [God] hath made [Christ] to be sin for us, who knew no sin; that we might be made the righteousness of God in him. (2 Cor 5:21)

This is what is referred to as the *"Great Exchange."* God applied unto Christ (who did not commit any sin) all of our sins, iniquities, disobedience, and transgressions. In the same manner, God applied unto us (who had no righteousness) all of Christ's goodness and righteousness. Through the cross, God gave us Christ's righteousness, which is called *justification*. One definition of the word *"justification"* is: *"just as if we have never sinned."*

This makes us righteous according to God's Word and worthy to claim, confess, and receive God's healing and blessings that are reserved for the righteous. So when you read scriptures that refer to the blessings of God belonging to the righteous, you can now claim those blessing for your life regardless of the sins of your past. You can claim them because, through Christ, you have become the seed of Abraham, heirs according to God's promises, a righteous child of God, and worthy to receive your healing.

Your True Self

The following is a prayer confession that I encourage you to pray from time to time. You are righteous in Christ and worthy to receive God's healing regardless of your past life of sin. *Hebrews 4:16* tells us to *come boldly before the throne of grace to receive our blessings.* You will not be able to release the faith you need to receive your healing if Satan can get you to come before God to request your healing with sin-consciousness. But when you come before God to request your healing with God-consciousness and Christ's righteousness, and you know in your heart that you are righteous by Christ, you can come before God with boldness in your heart and faith to receive your healing.

In the eyes of God, the true you is not your life of sins, failures, mistakes, and shortcomings. The true you (your true self) is the image of God in Christ and His righteousness (our true righteousness).

I encourage you to pray this prayer from time to time when you are making your healing confessions. It will encourage you to walk by faith in your righteousness in Christ and receive your divine healing.

MY TRUE SELF

Father in heaven, I thank You for giving Your Son, Jesus Christ to be my true self. He is the God-man. He is all God, who represents You, Father, and yet He is man, who represents me. He is the perfect man—Jesus Christ. He is the man of Your pleasure. He is the man of Your delight, and He is the man of Your joy. He is Your beloved Son, whom You have declared to the whole world that You are well pleased in Him.

Lord Jesus, when You went to the cross and suffered, bled, and died, You transformed me from myself to Yourself. I was transformed into Your image and Your reflection. The cross has become my mirrored reflection of You. When God looks at me now, He does not see me in my flesh or in my sins. He sees me in the sinless, righteous reflection of You.

I am hid in You, and all of my sinful works and deeds are covered by Your blood. Lord Jesus, I accept You now as my true self. You are my true identity. You are my true righteousness. You are my true holiness. You are my true goodness. And, Your works are my true good works.

Lord, You have declared in Your Word, that as You are, so am I in this world. I receive Your image and Your reflection of who I really am and who You are upon my life, spirit, and soul. And, I thank You that through the cross, You are the image that God sees of me. And, since He is well pleased with You, He is therefore well-pleased with me, because of Your sacrifice and because Your reflection and image is upon me.

Because You are my true self, I am not ashamed to come into Your presence. I am not ashamed to come before Your throne of grace to ask You for healing. And, because I am in Christ, and I am covered by His righteousness, I also boldly claim every promise of healing that You have reserved for the righteous children of God.

I come boldly before Your throne of grace as the seed of Abraham, a son, and an heir to the blessings of the Kingdom. I come boldly before You with a clear conscious in Christ, and as a righteous son with a blood-bought right to petition You for all things.

I receive You as my true self, my true reflection, my true image, and in my true position with the Father. In the name of Jesus Christ, I thank You, AMEN.

Chapter 7

Things That Can Hinder Our Healing

> *Ye have sown much, and bring in little; ye eat, but ye have not enough; ye drink, but ye are not filled with drink; ye clothe you, but there is none warm; and he that earneth wages earneth wages to put it into a bag with holes. Thus saith the LORD of hosts; Consider your ways. (Hag 1:6-7)*

This passage shows us that we can put forth positive work and effort for one thing, while at the same time nullifying our positive efforts through negative actions and works. Thus far, we have given several powerful, effective keys that are effective in establishing and bringing about our healing. However, there are some things that we can do that can become counterproductive to our work of faith, prayers, and confessions, and actually hinder our healing.

The wilderness experience was an example of this. The Israelites were constantly moving and traveling trying to get to the promised land; however, their lack of faith in God, as well as their sinful and rebellious deeds and behavior kept them wandering in the wilderness and going nowhere for 40 years. They did the right things on one hand, but on the other hand, they countered those things with their negative actions and works.

It's the same way with our healing. We can pray, confess the Word of God, and do the productive things that work towards our healing. But if we are not mindful, we can at the same time be doing things that counteract our spiritual works and hinder our healing from coming forth.

In Verse 7, God told the people why they were spinning their wheels and going nowhere. He told them that they need to consider their ways. It's like a tug of war. You can pull on one side (with doing the right things), but if you have someone resisting you on the other side and pulling in the opposite direction, you will go nowhere.

The following are five things the Bible clearly teaches that can hinder our healing. Examine yourself concerning these things and make sure that you are not guilty of spinning your wheels and going nowhere (with your healing).

1. Negative Words

Teach me, and I will hold my tongue: and cause me to understand wherein I have erred. How forcible are right words… (Job 6:24-25)

In the book of Job, Job discovered some mistakes he had made by speaking the wrong things. Through trial and error, he eventually learned from his mistakes and began asking God to help him to say the right things so that he wouldn't give any place to the devil.

The prayers of the righteous are powerful, effective, and unstoppable by Satan. However, Satan is very shrewd in an attempt to hinder our prayers. He knows that there is nothing that hinders our prayers like the sins of our mouth.

As we have discovered, our mouths are weapons of war against the devil. But in warfare, soldiers must take time to periodically clean their weapons. If they do not, gun powder residue will become built up in the chamber of their weapon and will cause a malfunction, or even worse, cause the weapon to backfire on the person and harm the shooter.

When we speak negative words, they do the exact same thing to us. They clog up the pathway to our blessings and cause our prayer requests to malfunction. The soldier who fires a weapon that is clogged up wonders why they are pulling the trigger and nothing is happening. It's the same with us. We can do all the right things in petitioning God concerning our healing (pulling the trigger), and yet nothing happens because our negative words have caused our weapon to malfunction.

Negative words consist of anything that counters what we believe God for. If you are believing God for a particular healing, never allow yourself to say anything that is contrary to what you are believing, regardless of how you feel. Always keep your weapon clean by speaking only positive words concerning your healing.

If you have been speaking words of doubt, fear and unbelief concerning your healing, clean your weapon by repenting of those words and begin speaking the right words concerning your healing.

Negative words that can clog up your weapon are things such as lying, gossiping, and backbiting. These things can easily sneak into our lives. Begin praying and asking God each day to help you guard your mouth from lying and other sins of the mouth so that your words would be acceptable in His sight.

If the enemy comes upon you and causes you to fall into one of these verbal pitfalls, don't just lie there and wallow in it. Be quick to repent and ask God to cleanse your heart and spirit so that you will be able to maintain a clean weapon and so that your prayers will not be hindered.

2. Unrepentant Sin

But your iniquities have separated between you and your God, and your sins have hid his face from you, that he will not hear. (Is 59:2)

This scripture shows us that sin separates us from God. If sin separates us from God, then sin automatically separates us from receiving God's blessings. James 1:15 tells us that sin causes a type of (little by little) death to our relationship with God. It's the same kind of death that God said would happen to Adam in the Garden of Eden. God promised them they would die if they disobeyed (sinned against) Him. They disobeyed and they died. It wasn't a physical death; it was a spiritual death. Spiritual death is a separation from God and a separation from God's blessings.

It's not one sin or even a particular type of sin that brings this kind of spiritual death. The kind of sin that brings this type of death is continual, unrepentant sin. God refers to this type of sin as a type of witchcraft. It's the kind of sin that the Holy Spirit has made a person aware of and brings to their mind and heart, but the person makes a conscious decision to rebel and continue in the sin without repentance or change.

The story of the prodigal son shows us that God is waiting to receive us and bless us even after we have sinned. All it takes to get back in the favor and blessings of God is true repentance. In this story, once the son repented, the father restored all he had lost.

If you have been doing everything you can do and have not received your healing, check your heart concerning sin in your life. Ask God to reveal all known sin to you. Repent of it totally and wholly. Then plead the blood of Jesus over your life. This opens you back up to receive God's blessings once again.

3. Unforgiveness

And forgive us our debts, as we forgive our debtors. (Mat 6:12)

Many people try to have a relationship with God without realizing that our relationship with God is tied in with our relationship with others. Jesus said that you cannot love Him without loving your brothers around you. In the above passage He ties our forgiveness in with us forgiving others. You cannot harbor unforgiveness in your heart towards others and receive forgiveness from God. They are completely tied together.

We discovered in the previous topic that sin will hinder our healing and blessings. If God does not forgive us, it will cause our sin to remain and, thus, hinder our healing. We also discovered that the way back to the blessings of God is to repent.

Repentance clears us of our wrongs (by the blood of Jesus Christ) and opens the door for us to once again receive God's blessings. But if we are not forgiven by God, then the sin remains and hinders us. It's a three-way triangle. We need God's healing and blessings. But in order to receive our healing, we must be forgiven by God, and to be forgiven by God, we must forgive our brethren.

When you realize that grudge holding and unforgiveness hinders you from receiving your blessing of healing, it makes it a little easier to release them and forgive them.

4. Anger and Contention with Others

Therefore if thou bring thy gift to the altar, and there rememberest that thy brother hath ought against thee; Leave there thy gift before the altar, and go thy way; first be reconciled to thy brother, and then come and offer thy gift. (Mat 5:23-24)

The above passage shows us that anger and contention with the brethren will hinder our prayers. In this passage, Jesus said that if you come to pray and remember that there is contention with someone in your life, to leave your gift and go and make it right with them. This must be done before God will answer our prayers.

What makes this passage even more difficult to swallow is that Jesus doesn't make a distinction of whose fault it was that started the contention. Regardless of whose fault it was, the hindrance is still there.

For many of us, this is one of the hardest things to do in the Bible. The spirit of pride does not want you to do this. It takes a humbling spirit to do it. But you must be more concerned about getting your heart right with God and receiving your healing than you are about whose fault it was and who started the contention.

If you attempt to go to them and they refuse to amend the situation, then you are released from it and God will then release your prayers to be answered and receive your blessings. All God requires you to do is to get your heart right concerning the matter.

5. Unbelief and a Lack of Faith

Then came the disciples to Jesus apart, and said, Why could not we cast him out? And Jesus said unto them, Because of your unbelief: for verily I say unto you, If ye have faith as a grain of mustard seed, ye shall say unto this mountain, Remove hence to yonder place; and it shall remove; and nothing shall be impossible unto you. (Mat 17:19-20)

In the above passage, Jesus' disciples were attempting to cast a devil out of a little boy but failed to do so. They later asked Jesus why they could not cast the devil out of the boy. Jesus answered and told them that it was because of their unbelief.

Unbelief comes when we become intimidated by our circumstances. It's like a big bully that causes fear because of their size or their words of intimidation. In the case of the disciples, it may have been because the demon acted in a way that intimidated them in their faith. The same thing can happen to us. We can become intimidated by the doctor's report, the pain, and the things we see and hear in the lives of other people regarding their healing.

The story of David and Goliath has shown us that size has nothing to do with your ability to overcome the enemy. David's faith was bigger than Goliath; therefore, his faith was able to defeat Goliath. Some people can easily believe that God can heal a headache. But when it comes to more overwhelming illnesses and diseases (Goliaths), many people become intimidated and hindered in their faith.

Our faith becomes built up by the Word of God. This is why we must continue to speak and stay in His Word. The more we stay in the Word, the more our faith becomes built up and established in God. Then, when the enemy comes against us as an overwhelming flood, the Spirit of God will raise up a standard against him. This standard is our faith and confidence that is unshakable and immovable in God. You can only get this kind of faith when you are steadfast and continually in God's Word.

Conclusion:

God has given us the ability to receive our healing by utilizing the measure of faith He has give us in conjunction with the power and authority of His Word. But even though we have all this power and authority behind us, there are pitfalls that can cause our faith and spiritual efforts toward our healing to be counterproductive.

Let us not give the devil any place to help him hinder our healing. Let us close the door to these things. Once they are closed, we can decree and declare our healing by the authority of God's Word without the hindering spirit of the enemy. And, we can thereafter, receive the blessing and manifestation of our healing.

―――― Chapter 8 ――――

Spiritual Warfare Prayer

Father, I come boldly before Your throne of grace thanking and praising You for the authority that You have given us to decree and declare healing over our bodies.

I ask for Your forgiveness for anything that I have done physically or spiritually to open a door or contribute to this affliction in any way. Forgive me for the things I've done knowingly, those which I have done unknowingly, and for those things which I may have omitted or neglected that may have brought this infirmity upon me. Father, by Your amazing grace, and by the power of the cross and blood of Jesus Christ, I receive Your forgiveness, cleansing, and wholeness in my spirit, soul, and body, in the name of Jesus Christ.

I speak to every demon, every devil, and every demonic spirit that is associated with this sickness or disease, and I command you to loose and release every grip, stronghold, and anchor from my body, and let my body go, in the name of Jesus Christ. I command every curse, every negative word, and every spirit of witchcraft that may be behind this infirmity to be canceled and to be inoperative and ineffective against my body. I command you to go back from where you came. For God has declared that no weapon that is formed against me shall prosper, and every negative word and curse that is spoken over or against my life or my body shall fall to the ground and be destroyed. I decree and declare this, in the name of Jesus Christ.

Lord, You have declared in Your Word that every knee shall bow and every tongue shall confess that Jesus Christ is Lord. Therefore, as I lift up the name of Jesus Christ, I command this sickness, disease and spirit of infirmity to bow to the authority, power and the name of Jesus Christ. And, I command you to loose every hold and grip from my body, leaving my body whole and healed in the name of Jesus Christ.

As Jesus commanded the storm to cease, and it obeyed Him and ceased, I command this storm of affliction and infirmity in my body to cease, now, and be still! I also command all storms of pain, agony, and severe discomfort in my body to also cease, now, in the name of Jesus Christ!

As Elijah called down fire to consume those that came against him, I call down the fire of the Holy Ghost to consume every unlawful thing that is in or upon my body. I call the fire of the Holy Ghost to burn up and consume every negative cell, bacteria, infection, and every harmful thing that is in or upon my body, by the authority of the name of Jesus Christ.

As Joshua and the children of Israel shouted and the walls of Jericho came down, I shout the name of Jesus Christ! And with the shout of His mighty name, I command every wall and defense of the enemy, and every stronghold spirit of infirmity in my life or in or upon my body to be broken down, crushed, and destroyed, in the name of Jesus Christ.

As Jesus cursed the fig tree and it died at the root, I curse every root of sickness and disease in or upon my body, and I command them to die at the root, and to be plucked up and out of my body, and never spring up again, in the name of Jesus Christ.

I command every infection of any kind in my blood and bloodstream to die and be swept away: that includes any infection or attack of my white blood cells, red blood cells, or any parts of blood. And, I command my blood, bloodstream, organs, and every system in my body to be purified and cleansed from all bacteria, infection, poison, or unlawful intrusion of any kind, by the purifying power of the blood of Jesus Christ and the power of the Holy Ghost.

I command every unlawful and harmful growth that may be in or upon any part my body to cease to grow, die, and dissolve. And, I command any trace of them to be totally and completely flushed out of my body and cast into the sea by the authority of the name of Jesus Christ.

Father, You have declared that You have given us the authority to speak life by the power of our words. Therefore, I speak strength and life unto my body, now! And, by the power of the name of Jesus Christ, I say be strong, be healed, and be made whole.

I decree that every blood test, x-ray, imaging scan, and every test result of any kind concerning my body to be corrected in my body by the power of the Holy Ghost. And, I command their functions to line up with God's Word concerning my body and begin operating at one-hundred percent efficiency and function and perform in perfection, in the manner in which God created them to operate and perform. In the name of Jesus Christ I decree and declare it.

Father, I thank You for the benefits that You have given

us through the sacrifice and blood of Jesus Christ. And Lord, I receive Your benefits into my life and body this day personally. For You have declared in Your Word that through Christ that You would forgive all of my iniquities, You would heal all of my sickness and diseases, You would redeem my life from every destruction and attack of the enemy, You would crown me with Your loving kindness and tender mercies, You would satisfy my life with Your blessings and good things, and You would renew the strength of my spirit, soul, and body like You renew the strength of the eagle. Father, You are the promise keeper; and by my faith in You and the promise of Your Word, I receive each and every one of these promises in my body; and as a result, I receive my complete wholeness and healing, in the name of Jesus Christ.

Lord, I give You praise and thanksgiving for the sufferings that You undertook for me so that I could receive my healing. By Your sufferings, You paid the price for my sins, transgressions, and iniquities. You also took many agonizing and painful stripes in order that I may be healed from sickness and diseases. And Lord, You did not take any of those stripes in vain. So I boldly decree and declare that *BY THE STRIPES* that You took upon Your body for me, that, *I AM HEALED!*

Now Father, I confess that nothing is too hard for You to do. Therefore, healing my body is nothing for You; for You are the Almighty God, with all power and might. So I give You all the glory, praise, honor, adoration, and thanksgiving in advance for touching and healing my body. In the name of the Lord, Jesus Christ, I decree and declare it. AMEN!

Chapter 9

Introduction to: Spiritual Warfare Healing Confessions

And ye shall take a bunch of hyssop, and dip it in the blood that is in the bason, and strike the lintel and the two side posts with the blood that is in the bason...
Exodus 12:22

In Exodus chapter 12, God gave the Israelites instructions to take the blood of the Passover Lamb (representing Jesus Christ), put it into a basin, and apply it to the lintel and doorposts (representing the cross) of each home, before they left Egypt.

If the blood of the lamb was given to a home in a basin and it was not applied to the lintel and doorposts, they would not have been covered and protected from the death angel.

Hyssop is a plant that grows about 2 feet in length. It has a strong woody stalk that enables it to stand up to brushing and being used for applications. It was often used for applying blood or oil in holy, sacred ceremonies.

Hyssop is what was used to apply the blood of the Passover Lamb that protected and delivered them. Without the application (using the hyssop to apply the blood), the blood (sitting in a basin) would not have done them any good.

Spiritually, hyssop is the application of the Word of God and the blood of Jesus Christ. As all-powerful as the Word of God and the blood of Jesus Christ is, they will do us no good if we do not apply them.

So hyssop represents the method of how we apply the blood of Jesus Christ and the Word of God to our lives. Although hyssop is the entire process of seeing, hearing, meditating upon, and speaking the Word of God, hyssop primarily represents us speaking (applying) the Word of God and the blood of Jesus Christ to our lives.

This chapter contains 160 healing scriptures and spiritual warfare healing confessions. They are the seeds of God's Word that pertain to your healing. The scripture passage before the confessions are your authority to utilize the Word of God. The confession after the scripture is what you use to personalize that seed for your life and bring the manifestation of God's healing.

Again, hyssop is the method or process of how we apply the Word of God and the blood of Jesus Christ to our lives. I encourage you to read and confess at least ten to twenty sets of them each day. God has declared in His Word in Romans 10:9 that *whatever we confess with our mouth and believe in our heart we shall receive*. As you speak and confess these scriptures and confessions, you will be using hyssop and applying God's Word and the blood of Jesus Christ to your life. Remember, it's the application of the Word of God and blood of Jesus Christ that mixes with your faith that produce the fruit (manifestation) of your healing.

Chapter 10

Spiritual Warfare Healing Confessions

> *Isaiah 53:3-5 He is despised and rejected of men; a man of sorrows, and acquainted with grief: and we hid as it were our faces from him; he was despised, and we esteemed him not. Surely he hath borne our griefs, and carried our sorrows: yet we did esteem him stricken, smitten of God, and afflicted. But he was wounded for our transgressions, he was bruised for our iniquities: the chastisement of our peace was upon him; and with his stripes we are healed.*

Confession: Surely, Jesus Christ has borne my sicknesses, diseases, and my pains. He took my sicknesses and diseases and carried them to the cross. When they nailed Jesus to the cross, they were also nailing my sicknesses and diseases to the cross. He bore them for me. Therefore, I do not have to bear them or carry them myself. I refuse to bear or carry what Jesus Christ bore and carried for me. Therefore, I decree and declare that by the stripes that Jesus Christ took for me, I am healed!

> *I Cor 19-20 What? Know ye not that your body is the temple of the Holy Ghost which is in you, which ye have of God, and ye are not your own? For ye are bought with a price: therefore glorify God in your body, and in your spirit, which are God's.*

Confession: God has made my body to be the temple of the Holy Spirit. He has also bought me with the price of His own blood. That makes my body God's property. So Satan, I decree and declare that you take your hands off of God's property. I command that you loose and let go of my body of all sickness, disease, and every spirit of infirmity, by the authority of the mighty name of Jesus Christ.

Pro 4:20-22 My son, attend to my words; incline thine ear unto my sayings. Let them not depart from thine eyes; keep them in the midst of thine heart. For they are life unto those that find them, and health to all their flesh.

Confession: I will give close and earnest attention to the Word of God, and I will listen carefully to what He says. I will not let His Word depart from my eyes; nor will I allow the Word to cease from coming forth from my mouth. I will treasure God's Word and keep it in the midst of my heart. For the Word of God brings life to my spirit. It is medicine to my body. It is restoration to my soul. It is full of the life of God. As I read and confess it, God's Word deposits the healing virtue and the life of God into my body that heals me and makes me whole.

3 John 2 Beloved, I wish above all things that thou mayest prosper and be in health, even as thy soul prospereth.

Confession: It is God's desire to bless and prosper me. By His grace, He blesses my soul to prosper in Him. Because my soul prospers in Him, He blesses me to prosper in my finances, my life, my family, and in my health.

Mark 5:25-29 And a certain woman, which had an issue of blood twelve years, and had suffered many things of many physicians, and had spent all that she had, and was nothing bettered, but rather grew worse; When she had heard of Jesus, came in the press behind, and touched his garment. For she said, if I may touch but his clothes, I shall be whole. And straightway the fountain of her blood was dried up; and she felt in her body that she was healed of that plague.

Confession: This woman with an issue of blood was made whole by her faith in God. I therefore reach forth supernaturally by my faith in God, and I touch the hem of Jesus' garment. And, as she pressed through the crowd, I likewise press through the hindrances and distractions in my life. I also press through every spiritual hindrance and hindering spirit of the enemy, and I touch Jesus. I touch Jesus by hearing, speaking, and confessing His Word. As I touch Him, I receive the healing virtue of the Holy Spirit.

Mark 10:27 And Jesus looking upon them saith, With men it is impossible, but not with God: for with God all things are possible.

Confession: According to man and doctors, many sicknesses and diseases are irreversible. They say that it is impossible to be healed of many of them. But they don't know my God. They don't know the power of the blood of Jesus Christ and the power of His Word. They may say that it is impossible, but I agree with God. And I declare that all things are possible to him that believes. And, since I am a believer, I receive the miraculous healing power of God manifested in my life and in my body.

Judges 15:14-16 And when [Samson] came unto Lehi, the Philistines shouted against him: and the Spirit of the LORD came mightily upon him, and the cords that were upon his arms became as flax that was burnt with fire, and his bands [were] loosed from off his hands... And he found a new jawbone of a [donkey], and he used it and slew a thousand Philistines with it.

Confession: God gave Samson supernatural strength to

slay the Philistines. Samson's strength did not come from his own might; it came from God's anointing. God has likewise given me supernatural strength through His anointing and His Word. And, with the strength and power of God's anointing and His Word, I likewise do so to the spiritual Philistines: I loose every stronghold of infirmity. I break their bands off from my body. I cast off every spirit of infirmity. I destroy every yoke of sickness and disease, and I decree that I am healed by the power and the anointing of the Lord.

Heb 12:29 For our God is a consuming fire.

Confession: By the authority of Jesus Christ, I release the consuming fire of the Holy Spirit in and through my body to consume everything that is causing this affliction. May God's presence consume every negative and destructive germ, bacteria, infection, cell, and every harmful thing in or on my body that is contributing to this affliction. May the radiant fire of the Holy Spirit burn and consume every one of them, so they will no longer exist in or on my body. I decree this by the authority of the name of Jesus Christ.

Luke 1:38 And Mary said, Behold the handmaid of the Lord; be it unto me according to thy word....

Confession: Mary supernaturally received the seed of God (Jesus Christ) through her faith, her openness, and her receptivity to the Word of God which was spoken unto her. I therefore open up my heart unto God, and by my faith, I receive God's seed of healing. And I say to You, O Lord, let Your healing be manifested in my body according to Your Word.

Mark 16:17-18 And these signs shall follow them that believe; In my name shall they cast out devils; they shall speak with new tongues; they shall take up serpents; and if they drink any deadly thing, it shall not hurt them; they shall lay hands on the sick, and they shall recover.

Confession: I am a believer. I have believed and received the Lord, Jesus Christ into my heart and life. God has declared that His miraculous signs shall follow me as a believer. So in the name of Jesus Christ, these signs follow me: I cast out devils; I speak with new tongues; and I lay hands upon the sick and the sick recover. So by the authority of the name of Jesus Christ, I lay hands on myself, and I declare my wholeness, healing, and health, by the power of His name.

Rom 3:4 ...let God be true, but every man a liar....

Confession: Jesus Christ is the way, the truth, and the life. His Word is the only truth there is. What the Word of God has declared about my healing is the truth. Everything else is a lie. Therefore, sickness and disease is just a manifested lie. Every negative doctor's report, pain, and infirmity concerning my body is a manifested lie. Jesus has declared that the truth of God's Word counteracts and sets us free from the manifested lies of the devil. Therefore, as I speak and stand on the truth of God's Word concerning my healing, every manifested lie of sickness and disease is cast down and destroyed, I am set free, and I receive the manifested truth of God's healing in my body.

Luke 24:36 And as they thus spake, Jesus himself stood in the midst of them, and saith unto them, Peace be unto you.

Confession: Shalom is a Hebrew word that means peace. Shalom also means completeness, as well as wholeness in health and well-being. When Jesus spoke Shalom unto His disciples, He was also speaking unto me as a disciple of Christ. I therefore receive the Shalom of God into my life, and I also receive the Shalom of God of complete healing and wholeness in my health and in my body.

> *1 John 5:4 For whatsoever is born of God overcometh the world: and this is the victory that overcometh the world, even our faith.*

Confession: Jesus Christ overcame the world. He also overcame the temptations, trials, and tests of this world. God has given me the power through Christ to also be an overcomer. Therefore, I declare that I am an overcomer of this infirmity through the power of Jesus Christ, my Lord.

> *Deut 30:19, Prov 18:21, 12:18: I call heaven and earth to record this day against you, that I have set before you life and death, blessing and cursing: therefore choose life, that both thou and thy seed may live; * Death and life are in the power of the tongue: and they that love it shall eat the fruit thereof; * The tongue of the wise is health.*

Confession: God breathed the breath of life into man. With the breath of life, man became a living soul and a speaking spirit in the image of God. God has also given us the authority and power of a speaking spirit to speak death or life to our circumstances and situations. I therefore choose to speak life and health to my body.

According to God's Word, I can have whatsoever I speak. So I speak with the authority of Christ, and I decree life, health, healing, restoration, and wholeness unto my body. There is healing in the power of my words. The words of my mouth make me whole. I speak and agree with what God has spoken concerning my healing. Therefore, I say that no plague or sickness can continue to dwell upon my body any longer. I say that it has to leave, now! I say that it has to go and depart from my body, now! I say that every infirmity is off limits to my body and must leave my body and be cast into the sea, now! I speak to every cell, organ, fiber, and every part of my body, and I speak life, wholeness, and health, in the name of Jesus Christ.

> *I John 3:8 He that committeth sin is of the devil; for the devil sinneth from the beginning. For this purpose the Son of God was manifested, that he might destroy the works of the devil.*

Confession: Sin is a work of the devil. Sickness and disease are also works of the devil. Jesus came to destroy all the works of the devil. Jesus accomplished His task and destroyed the works of the devil in the earth and in my life, through the power of the cross. Jesus has destroyed and annihilated sin, sickness, and disease from my life and my body. Therefore, I confess that this infirmity upon my body is destroyed by the works of Jesus Christ, and I therefore claim my healing.

> *Isaiah 65:24 And it shall come to pass, that before they call, I will answer; and while they are yet speaking, I will hear.*

Confession: My God is not dead; He is alive. He is not deaf; He hears the prayers and cries of His people. He hears me when I call and cry unto Him. He answers me and shows me great and mighty things, and He gives unto me His great blessings, prosperity, and healing. And, as I have cried out unto Him concerning this infirmity, I rejoice in my faith in Him that He has already heard me. And by my faith, I know that He has already healed and delivered me.

> *Luk 4:18-19 The Spirit of the Lord is upon me, because he hath anointed me to preach the gospel to the poor; he hath sent me to heal the brokenhearted, to preach deliverance to the captives, and recovering of sight to the blind, to set at liberty them that are bruised; to preach the acceptable year of the Lord.*

Confession: God anointed Jesus Christ with the fullness of His Spirit, power and might. Jesus was sent by God to heal our broken hearts, to set free those who have been taken captive by the enemy with strongholds and bondages, to bring illumination to our spirits and spiritual eyes, to reveal to us the truth of the mysteries of the gospel, to heal the sick and give sight to the blind, and to preach that *now* is the acceptable year of the Lord. Therefore, through the death, burial, and resurrection of Jesus Christ, we sound the trumpets and proclaim our victory, that this is *(now)* the year of Jubilee, the day of our salvation, and the hour of our healing and deliverance.

Eph 1:19 And what is the exceeding greatness of his power to us-ward who believe, according to the working of his mighty power.

Confession: Great and mighty is the Lord. His mighty power is exceedingly great. Through Christ, God has given me the power to overcome all sickness and disease. This power is unstoppable, irresistible, and greater than any sickness or disease. This power is flowing in and through me, healing me now and making me whole.

Mark 4:39 And he arose, and rebuked the wind, and said unto the sea, Peace, be still. And the wind ceased, and there was a great calm.

Confession: By the power of His Word, Jesus rebuked the raging wind and sea and commanded them to be at peace and be still, and they obeyed Him and were calm and at rest. Jesus has also given me the power and authority to use His name to rebuke the raging winds and storms in my life. So, by the power and the authority of the name of Jesus Christ, I rebuke this raging storm of infirmity in my body. I rebuke all pain, irritation, soreness, and discomfort, and I command my body to be at peace and be still, calm, and at rest, in the mighty name of Jesus Christ.

John 15:4-5 Abide in me, and I in you. As the branch cannot bear fruit of itself, except it abide in the vine; no more can ye, except ye abide in me. I am the vine, ye are the branches: He that abideth in me, and I in him, the same bringeth forth much fruit: for without me ye can do nothing.

Confession: Christ is my all and all. He is my true source for everything. He is the true and living vine, and I am one of His branches. He is my Jehovah-Jireh — the Lord God my provider. He is the Great "I AM." He is everything I need in my life; for everything that I need is provided through Him — my true vine. Because I am linked and connected to Him, what flows through Him flows in me. Therefore, blessings flow through Him unto me. Prosperity flows through Him unto me. I also receive the healing power that is in and through Him flowing to my body and through my body making me whole.

Matt 8:16 When the even was come, they brought unto him many that were possessed with devils: and he cast out the spirits with his word, and healed all that were sick.

Confession: God is the same yesterday, today, and forever. Over two thousand years ago, Jesus used the power of His Word to cast out demons and devils and spirits of infirmity from all the people. Today, He has the same power and authority to cast them out. Christ has also given us the power of His Word to cast out demons and devils and spirits of infirmity. So, by the power and the authority of the Word of the living God, I cast this spirit of infirmity out of my body.

Num 21:8-9 And the LORD said unto Moses, Make thee a fiery serpent, and set it upon a pole: and it shall

> *come to pass, that every one that is bitten, when he looketh upon it, shall live. And Moses made a serpent of brass, and put it upon a pole, and it came to pass, that if a serpent had bitten any man, when he beheld the serpent of brass, he lived.*

Confession: The serpent represents my sins and iniquities. The brass represents God's judgment. The pole represents the cross. Just as God provided healing for the Israelites in the wilderness though a picture of the cross in this example, He has provided healing for me through the real, true cross of Jesus Christ. Praise and glory be unto God for His loving-kindness and tender mercies toward us. Through His love and grace, He allowed His only Son to be brutally nailed to the cross for my sins, sicknesses, and diseases. And God has declared that anyone who looks unto Jesus Christ and the power of the cross would be healed. Therefore, I look unto my Lord, Jesus Christ and the deliverance of the cross, and I receive life, healing, and restoration in my body.

> *Mat 8:5-13 …there came unto Him a centurion, beseeching Him, and saying, Lord, my servant lieth at home sick of the palsy, grievously tormented. And Jesus saith unto him, I will come and heal him… The centurion answered and said… speak the word only, and my servant shall be healed… And Jesus said unto the centurion, Go thy way; and as thou hast believed, so be it done unto thee. And his servant was healed in the selfsame hour.*

Confession: I believe in the power of the Word of God. I believe the Word of God contains the life of God to heal me. I choose to therefore speak the Word of God. I will not speak that which is contrary to the Word of God, but I will *"speak the Word only."* I will speak only what the Word of God says concerning my healing. And, as I believe according to the Word concerning my healing, it shall be done unto me.

> *Mark 1:34 And Jesus healed many who had various diseases. He also drove out many demons, but he would not let the demons speak because they knew who he was. (NIV)*

Confession: Jesus has authority over all demons, devils, evil spirits, and spirits of infirmity. He drives them out by His power and might. He commands them and even forbids them to speak. Jesus has also given us the power and authority to command them in His name. I therefore forbid the spirit of infirmity from continuing to cause destruction, illness, or disease upon my body. I command every germ, disease, infection, and virus to die instantly and to cease to exist in or upon my body. And, I command my body to rise up and be healed, in the name of Jesus Christ.

> *Ezek 37:1-10 The hand of the LORD was upon me, and carried me out in the spirit of the LORD, and set me down in the midst of the valley which was full of bones... [Then] He said unto me, prophesy upon these bones, and say unto them, O ye dry bones, hear the word of the LORD... Thus saith the Lord GOD unto these bones; Behold, I will cause breath to enter into you, and ye shall live. So I prophesied as I was commanded: and as I prophesied, there was a noise, and behold a shaking, and the bones came together, bone to his bone... and the flesh came up upon them, and the skin covered them... and the breath came into them, and they lived, and stood up upon their feet, an exceeding great army.*

Confession: The Lord is the source of all life. He is the giver and sustainer of all life. He spoke and gave life to man and to all the living creatures upon the face of the earth. There is healing and life in the prophetic, spoken

Word of God. The Lord commanded Ezekiel to prophesy and speak life to dry bones and they obeyed him and came to life. The Lord has also given us the authority and power of His Word to speak and prophesy to the dry places of our lives. So I prophesy to the dry places of my body, which is this infirmity, and I say unto you, hear the Word of the Lord: receive the life of God into your bones, receive the life of God into your flesh, and receive the life-giving breath of God and be strengthened, revived, renewed, made whole, and be healed, in the name of Jesus Christ.

Ps 40:1-2 ...I waited patiently for the LORD; and he inclined unto me, and heard my cry. He brought me up also out of an horrible pit, out of the miry clay, and set my feet upon a rock, and established my goings.

Confession: As I patiently, consistently, and diligently speak and confess the Word of God concerning my healing, He inclines unto me and hears my cry. He rescues me and brings me out of a horrible pit of affliction. He delivers me out of the miry clay of infirmity. He establishes my feet upon the solid rock of His salvation and His Word, and He brings my healing into manifestation.

Ps 121:5-7 The LORD is thy keeper: the LORD is thy shade upon thy right hand. The sun shall not smite thee by day, nor the moon by night. The LORD shall preserve thee from all evil: he shall preserve thy soul.

Confession: The Lord is my sun and my shield. He is my great protector. He keeps me from falling, and presents me faultless before the presence of His glory with exceeding joy. He preserves my soul. He preserves me from all evil. He preserves and protects me from all the attacks of the enemy, physically and spiritually. The Lord even protects me from the sicknesses and diseases of this world. He rebukes them from my life and body. He blesses me with His complete shadow of protection because of Christ Jesus, our Lord.

Ps 147:3 He healeth the broken in heart, and bindeth up their wounds.

Confession: When my heart is scarred or wounded with the hurts and sorrows of this world, the Lord encourages my heart and lifts me up. When I am sad or lonely, the Lord comforts me and gives me His strength and joy. When I am heavily laden and overwhelmed with the problems and cares of this world, He removes the burden from me, and lightens my load. When my body is afflicted with sickness or disease, He touches me with His healing anointing, binds up my wounds, and makes me whole.

Heb 8:12 For I will be merciful to their unrighteousness, and their sins and their iniquities will I remember no more.

Confession: Because of the shed blood and the sacrifice of Jesus Christ, the Lord removes all of my sins and iniquities. He removes them from me as far as the east is from the west, never to return again and never to be remembered by Him. Because He removes all of my sins and iniquities, He also removes all of my sicknesses and diseases. Therefore I decree and declare that by the wounds and stripes of Jesus Christ, that the Lord has fully redeemed me, and I am whole and completely healed in my body.

Lam 3:22-23 It is of the LORD'S mercies that we are not consumed, because his compassions fail not. They are new every morning: great is thy faithfulness.

Confession: The Lord's mercies for us are steadfast and never ceasing. Each and every day He renews His goodness and mercies for us because of His faithfulness. It is because of the Lord's abundant mercies that He keeps us from being consumed. Therefore, I shall not be consumed by this affliction, and I shall be healed and fully recover.

> *Ps 107:20 He sent his word, and healed them, and delivered them from their destructions.*

Confession: The Lord sends blessings from the heavens to the earth to those who are called by His name. He sends His Word of deliverance to them. And for those who are afflicted, He sends His Word of healing to them.

> *Luke 18:8 I tell you that he will avenge them speedily. Nevertheless when the Son of man cometh, shall he find faith on the earth?*

Confession: The Lord is not slack or slow concerning His promise of healing. As we release faith in Him, speak His Word, and call upon His name, He answers us speedily, and He expedites His Word of healing and deliverance on our behalf.

> *Mat 7:7 Ask, and it shall be given you; seek, and ye shall find; knock, and it shall be opened unto you: For every one that asketh receiveth; and he that seeketh findeth; and to him that knocketh it shall be opened.*

Confession: The Lord is faithful to His children that call upon Him. As I call upon the Lord, He answers me. When I ask of Him, He freely gives me what I need. When I seek His face, He reveals unto me the glory of His blessings. When I knock, He opens the door and allows me to come into the green pastures of His blessings of abundance. As I have asked, knocked, and sought the Lord for my healing, He is faithful to heal me. For the blessings of the Lord are mine for the asking.

> *Rom 13:12 The night is far spent, the day is at hand: let us therefore cast off the works of darkness, and let us put on the armour of light.*

Confession: By the authority of Jesus Christ, I cast off every work of darkness from my body. I command every sickness and disease and spirit of infirmity to leave my body, now! Satan, take your hands off of my body, now! I cast you out, now, in the name of Jesus Christ!

> *Phil 2:10-11 That at the name of Jesus every knee should bow, of things in heaven, and things in earth, and things under the earth; And that every tongue should confess that Jesus Christ is Lord, to the glory of God the Father.*

Confession: Jesus Christ is Lord of all. Because of His power, authority, and Lordship, everything has to submit unto Him and bow before His name and His presence. Therefore, by the authority and power that He has given unto me, I command this sickness and spirit of infirmity to bow to the authority and anointing of the name of Jesus Christ, and be loosed from my body.

> *1 John 4:17 Herein is our love made perfect, that we may have boldness in the day of judgment: because as he is, so are we in this world.*

Confession: My sins, sicknesses, and diseases were put upon Christ when He was nailed to the cross. But God has raised Christ, our Savior, from the dead in His healed, whole, and incorruptible body. Because God has raised Him whole, there is now no sickness or disease upon Christ's body. God's Word has declared that as Christ is now, so am I now in my body in this world. Therefore, I decree and declare that as Christ is now (with no sickness or disease in His body), that so am I in this world (healed and delivered by God's power) with no sickness or disease in my body.

> *Heb 4:14 Seeing then that we have a great high priest, that is passed into the heavens, Jesus the Son of God, let*

us hold fast our profession.

Confession: Jesus Christ, the Son of God is my high priest. He has given me instructions in His Word to hold fast to the confession of my faith. My faith in Christ is my profession. His Word is my constant confession. Therefore, I will not be moved. I will stand steadfast in my confession and profession of faith concerning my healing. And He shall bring me through.

Isaiah 43:26 Put me in remembrance: let us plead together: declare thou, that thou mayest be justified.

Confession: God has told us to put Him in remembrance. So Father, first, I put You in remembrance of what Your Son, our Lord Jesus Christ, went through on the cross to redeem and deliver me from sickness and disease. For You have said (because of Christ) that You would be merciful unto us, and You would not remember our sins anymore. Secondly, I also put You in remembrance of Your Word that has declared that with the stripes of Jesus Christ, I am healed.

Matthew 8:2-3 And, behold, there came a leper and worshipped him, saying, Lord, if thou wilt, thou canst make me clean. And Jesus put forth his hand, and touched him, saying, I will; be thou clean. And immediately his leprosy was cleansed.

Confession: It is God's will and purpose for me to be healed. God is not stopping my healing. He has already released my healing. He is at work in me now to will and do His good pleasure of healing my body.

Joel 3:10 ... let the weak say, I am strong.

Confession: God created all things by the power of His Word. He has created me in His likeness. He has given me His authority to speak life to my world and my circumstances. So by my authority as a speaking spirit in the image of God, I speak life. By my words, I speak healing. I say that I am strong in the Lord and in the power of His might. I say that I am well and whole in my spirit, soul, and body. And I say that I am totally healed by the stripes of Jesus Christ.

Luke 3:5 Every valley shall be filled, and every mountain and hill shall be brought low; and the crooked shall be made straight, and the rough ways shall be made smooth.

Confession: Jesus came to make all things new. He came to set things in order that were misaligned through the fall of Adam. He came to destroy the works of the devil—including sickness and disease. By the authority of the name of Jesus Christ, I decree that the crooked things in my body (sickness and disease) must be made straight (which is healed), and the rough areas of my body (which is pain and discomfort) must be made smooth (released from my body) by the power of the Holy Spirit.

Joshua 3:10 And Joshua said, Hereby ye shall know that the living God is among you, and that he will without fail drive out from before you the Canaanites, and the Hittites, and the Hivites, and the Perizzites, and the Girgashites, and the Amorites, and the Jebusites.

Confession: The LORD is the Almighty God. The LORD is strong and mighty. The LORD is mighty in battle. He is with me as a mighty warrior. He is my battle-axe. He is my Captain in charge. He is my great warrior and my deliverer. He shall surely heal and deliver me from this affliction. Just as God anointed Joshua to drive out the inhabitants of the land, as I speak the Word of God, the Lord shall drive this infirmity far from my body without fail with His strong arm and His mighty power.

Ps 103:2-5 Bless the Lord, O my soul, and forget not all his benefits: Who forgiveth all thine iniquities; who healeth all thy diseases. Who redeemeth thy life from destruction; who crowneth thee with lovingkindness and tender mercies; Who satisfieth thy mouth with good things; so that thy youth is renewed like the eagle's.

Confession: I will bless the Lord continually from the depths of my soul. And I will command everything that is within me to bless Him, and bless His wonderful, holy, mighty, and majestic name. The Lord is the One who forgives me of all of my sins, iniquities, transgressions, and failures. He heals all of my sicknesses and diseases. He has redeemed my life, soul, and body from sickness and the grave. He has overshadowed me with His loving-kindness and His tender mercies. He feeds me with the goodness of His Word and His blessings; and He renews my life, health, and strength like He renews the strength of the eagle.

Nah 1:9 What do ye imagine against the LORD? He will make an utter end: affliction shall not rise up the second time.

Confession: By God's grace, He has put an utter end to this affliction and attack against my body. He has healed and made me whole. And, by the authority of the Word of the Lord, I decree and declare that this affliction shall not be able to come upon me a second time. It is prohibited and off limits from ever rising or coming upon my body again.

Gal 3:13 Christ hath redeemed us from the curse of the law, being made a curse for us: for it is written, Cursed is every one that hangeth on a tree.

Confession: Thanks be to God for His unspeakable gift of Jesus Christ, who has redeemed and delivered me from the curse of the law. Instead of the curse of hell, He has given me the glory of heaven and eternal life. Instead of the curse of sickness and disease, He has given me health and healing. Praise God! Christ has redeemed me from the curse. Praise God! Through Christ, I am set free and delivered from all the curses that are written within the law as a penalty of disobedience. For Christ became the curse for me. He took my curse. He took my penalty. He took my punishment. He was nailed to the cross in my place. Therefore, through the redemptive work of Christ, I am free from every curse of sickness and disease, and I am healed, in the name of Jesus Christ.

> *Col 1:13-14 Who hath delivered us from the power of darkness, and hath translated us into the kingdom of his dear Son: In whom we have redemption through his blood, even the forgiveness of sins....*

Confession: Through the power of the blood of Jesus Christ, I have been delivered from the power and authority of darkness. I have been forgiven of my sins. I have been delivered from Satan's power of sickness and disease. I have been transformed unto the power of God's Kingdom through Christ. The Kingdom of God has come unto us. The power of the Kingdom of God now resides within me. And, by the power of the Kingdom of God, I cast this spirit of infirmity out of and off my body in the mighty name of Jesus Christ.

> *Zec 3:2 And the LORD said unto Satan, The LORD rebuke thee, O Satan; even the LORD that hath chosen Jerusalem rebuke thee...*

Confession: It is the Lord who has rebuked Satan from my life and my body. Therefore, I stand on the authority of what God has spoken, and I agree with the Lord's rebuke. I declare, Satan, that you are rebuked from my body and my health, by the rebuke of the Most High God.

> *Mat 6:10 Thy kingdom come. Thy will be done in earth, as it is in heaven.*

Confession: Through Christ Jesus, the power of the Kingdom of heaven has come unto *(made available to)* us. Jesus has declared God's will to be done on earth as it is done in heaven. I stand in agreement with Christ and declare His will to be done on earth, and in my body and life as it is done in heaven. And, since there is no sickness or disease in heaven, I decree and declare sickness and disease to also be prohibited and off limits to my body here on earth.

> *Ps 42:11 Why art thou cast down, O my soul? and why art thou disquieted within me? Hope thou in God: for I shall yet praise him, who is the health of my countenance, and my God.*

Confession: I refuse to be cast down or discouraged because of this attack against my body. I also refuse to be worried or anxious over this attack. My hope is not in doctors, medicines, or treatments; my hope is in God—the one who is my true healer. He is the lifter of my head and my countenance, the encourager of my soul, and the healer of my body. Therefore, my lips shall praise Him, and I will give Him glory and bless Him as long as I shall live.

> *2 Th 1:11 Wherefore also we pray always for you, that our God would count you worthy of this calling, and fulfil all the good pleasure of his goodness, and the work of faith with power:*

Confession: Through the blood of Jesus Christ, God has counted me worthy to be a partaker of the inheritance of His grace and blessings. By Him, I am counted worthy, qualified, and entitled to receive His blessings and His grace of healing and wholeness in my body.

> *Luke 10:19 Behold, I give unto you power to tread on serpents and scorpions, and over all the powers of the enemy: and nothing shall by any means hurt you.*

Confession: Jesus has given me authority and power over

all the powers of the enemy. By the authority of God in Christ, I trample over all the powers of the devil. I trample over sickness and disease. I trample over every spirit of infirmity. And, by the power that Christ has given unto me, I decree and declare that this infirmity cannot continue to cause me pain, sickness, or hurt me in any way.

> *Eph 2:4-6 But God, who is rich in mercy, for his great love wherewith he loved us... hath quickened us together with Christ... And hath raised us up together, and made us sit together in heavenly places in Christ Jesus.*

Confession: Through the abundance of God's grace and mercy, He has made me to be alive in Christ. He has raised me up and joined me together with Him. God has also made me to be seated with Christ in heavenly places; therefore, I stand on top (in Christ), in my place of victory, with all things under my feet. I therefore declare that sickness and disease are defeated in my life and in my body, and they are under my feet!

> *Rom 4:15 ...for where no law is, there is no transgression.*

Confession: Through the blood of Jesus Christ, God has redeemed and freed me from the penalty of the law of sin and transgression. They have all been washed away, cleansed, and paid for by the blood of Jesus Christ and the cross. Since there is now no sin or transgression against me, it is hereby unlawful for the devil to put sickness or disease upon me. Therefore, I decree and declare sickness and disease to be unlawful against my body, and by the power of the blood of Jesus Christ, I proclaim that *I am healed!*

> *Mark 7:27 But Jesus said unto her, Let the children first be filled: for it is not meet to take the children's bread [which is their healing], and to cast it unto the*

dogs [the unbelievers and those who are out of covenant with God].

Confession: Through Christ, I am a child of God. Therefore, the promises and blessings of God are mine. They belong to me as a child of God. God's healing bread (which is my healing) belongs to me. I have a blood-bought right to be healed. It is part of my inheritance and redemptive right given to me through the blood covenant of Christ. Therefore I claim it; I eat of it freely; I am filled; and I am healed.

2 Cor 4:18 While we look not at the things which are seen, but at the things which are not seen: for the things which are seen are temporal; but the things which are not seen are eternal.

Confession: I do not look at or focus on the things that are seen (the circumstances with my body). Instead, I choose to look at and focus my attention on the things that are not seen (my healing, according to the Word of God). For the situation with my body is only temporary, and it is subject to change. But the spiritual things that I have spoken over my body (the Word of God) have been established by God, and shall come to pass.

John 19:30 When Jesus therefore had received the vinegar, he said, It is finished: and he bowed his head, and gave up the ghost.

Confession: Jesus completed all the work the Father had assigned Him to do in the earth. Part of His assignment was to destroy all the works of the enemy, which includes the evil work of sickness and disease. Jesus destroyed sickness and disease on the cross. He completely finished this assignment. I therefore receive the finished and completed work of Jesus of healing my body, and I speak and agree with the Word that Jesus declared on the cross: "It (*my healing*) is finished (which is *fully completed*)."

> 2 Cor 10:4-5 *(For the weapons of our warfare are not carnal, but mighty through God to the pulling down of strong holds;) Casting down imaginations, and every high thing that exalteth itself against the knowledge of God, and bringing into captivity every thought to the obedience of Christ;*

Confession: The weapons of my warfare are powerful and mighty through God in Christ. Through my weapons, I pull down every stronghold of sickness and disease from my life and from my body. I cast down every high power of darkness that attempts to fight against the power of God in my life to heal me. I cast down every imagination of the devil that wars against my faith—that includes every spirit of doubt, fear, and unbelief concerning my healing. I bring into captivity every negative, discouraging, and despairing thought concerning my healing to the obedience of Christ and the Word of God.

> *Isa 49:25 But thus saith the LORD...for I will contend with him that contendeth with thee....*

Confession: The Lord shall contend with all those that fight against and contend with me. And since this sickness contends with me, the Lord shall contend with it, and He shall surely fight on my behalf against this sickness and completely destroy it.

> *1 Peter 2:24 Who his own self bare our sins in his own body on the tree, that we, being dead to sins, should live unto righteousness: by whose stripes ye were healed.*

Confession: Jesus took and carried my sins, sicknesses, and diseases to the cross. He bore them on His own body when He was nailed to the cross (the tree). He took stripes (painful whips) upon His body so that I would be healed. Jesus did not take them in vain. He took them for the sins, sicknesses, and diseases of the world, but He also took them for me personally. And, because of the stripes that He took for me, I am healed. I accept and receive His payment for my forgiveness of sins and for my healing and deliverance. Therefore, by my faith in Jesus Christ and His redemptive work, I receive my healing.

Ps 62:6 [The Lord] only is my rock and my salvation: he is my defence; I shall not be moved.

Confession: The Lord is the rock of my salvation. He is unmovable and cannot be shaken. In Him do I steadfastly put my faith and trust. I stand strong in the Lord and in His Word. Because He is unmovable and I abide in Him, I stand unmovable in Him. I stand firmly in my faith and in my place of victory for my healing, and I refuse to be moved.

James 4:7 Submit yourselves therefore to God. Resist the devil, and he will flee from you.

Confession: I submit myself unto God. I submit myself to the will of God and the Word of God. I also submit myself unto the authority of God and His Word. Therefore, devil, I resist you! I resist sickness and disease! You cannot touch my body any longer! I command you to remove sickness and disease from my body! I command you to loose your hold upon my body and flee, now, in the name of Jesus Christ.

2 Cor 1:20 For all the promises of God in him [are] yea, and in him Amen, unto the glory of God by us.

Confession: I believe that the promises that God has given us in His Word are true. I release my faith in the promises of the Word of God. I don't have to wait until I see them manifested because I know that they are true. I therefore say *Amen* to the glory of God for the promises of His Word concerning my healing.

Ephesians 4:27 Neither give place to the devil.

Confession: I refuse to give any place to the devil. I refuse to give any place to sickness or disease in my life. I give no place with my words; for with my words I decree and declare that I am healed. I give no place with my faith; for with my faith I believe and know that I am healed. I give no place with my mind; for with mind I meditate upon my healing according to God's Word. I give no place with my heart; for with my heart I receive my healing according to the Word. Therefore, I close every door and access of the devil to my life. And, I thereby open the door through my faith and confession for the full manifestation of the Holy Spirit for my healing.

Gal 3:29 And if ye be Christ's, then are ye Abraham's seed, and heirs according to the promise.

Confession: Through the sacrifice of the cross, God has made me to be the seed of Abraham and an heir according to the promises. Healing is one of the promises that God gave to Abraham and his descendents. I claim my inheritance and my right to be healed as a seed of Abraham. It is mine. I receive it. I stand upon it. And, I therefore receive the inherited promise of my healing.

Mat 16:18 And I say also unto thee, That thou art Peter, and upon this rock I will build my church; and the gates of hell shall not prevail against it.

Confession: Jesus Christ is the Chief Cornerstone and the Rock of our salvation. God has built the church and established it upon the solid Rock of Jesus Christ. Therefore, the gates of hell cannot prevail against the church. And, since I am in Christ, and part of the church which God has established in Christ Jesus, I decree and declare that the gates of hell cannot prevail against me with this sickness or disease. And because Jesus is my Rock, I declare that I shall prevail over this infirmity.

> *Rom 12:2 And be not conformed to this world: but be ye transformed by the renewing of your mind, that ye may prove what is that good, and acceptable, and perfect will of God.*

Confession: I refuse to allow my mind and heart to become conformed to the doubt, fear, and unbelief of this world concerning the Word of God. My heart is fixed on believing and receiving the Word of God. And, as His Word is planted within my heart, His Word transforms my mind, body, and soul into His image, His life, and His mind. His Word also transforms the condition of my body to health and wholeness, as He manifests His good, acceptable, and perfect will in my life.

> *Mark 5:30 And Jesus, immediately knowing in himself that virtue had gone out of him, turned him about in the press, and said, Who touched my clothes?*

Confession: Jesus is full of the virtue of God. By my faith and my confession of the Word of God, I reach out and touch Jesus. And, by my touch of Christ, I receive the healing virtue flowing from Him unto my body, healing me and making me well.

> *Acts 10:38 How God anointed Jesus of Nazareth with the Holy Ghost and with power: who went about doing good, and healing all that were oppressed of the devil; for God was with him.*

Confession: God has anointed Jesus Christ with the Holy Ghost and with all power. The power of Christ has delivered and translated me from the powers of darkness. God has delivered me from all oppressions of the devil. This includes all oppressions of sicknesses and diseases. I have been, therefore, delivered from the authority of Satan and from all sickness and disease through the power of the

Holy Ghost.

> *Rom 8:37 Nay, in all these things we are more than conquerors through him that loved us.*

Confession: Jesus conquered and triumphed over Satan, sin, sickness, and disease. Through His death, burial, and resurrection, He has also given me the power to triumph over them. I am in Christ and Christ is in me. And, since I dwell in Christ, that also makes me more than a conqueror through Him. I therefore declare that I am a victorious conqueror over this infirmity through the power of my victorious Captain of the host of the armies of the Lord, Jesus Christ.

> *Jer 1:12 ...for I will hasten my word to perform it.*

Confession: When I speak the Word of God, the Lord hastens (speeds up) His Word to perform it on my behalf. He moves quickly to perform it because it's His Word. For He is not slow concerning the promise of His Word toward us. He therefore answers us speedily and expedites the performance of His Word on my behalf concerning my healing.

> *Num 23:8 How shall I curse, whom God hath not cursed, or how shall I defy, whom the LORD hath not defied?*

Confession: God has declared His canopy of protection and blessings upon my life. He has placed them in a hedge all around me on every side. Since the Lord has declared me to be blessed, I declare that I am blessed. I therefore declare that the curse of sickness and disease cannot stay upon my body. It cannot remain. It has to go, now! For Satan cannot curse what God has blessed.

> *Rom 10:17 So then faith cometh by hearing, and hearing by the word of God.*

Confession: I set myself to hear God's Word continually. The more I hear God's Word, the more His Word produces faith in my heart and my life. The more I am filled with faith in His Word, the more His Word comes alive within me, and the more my faith produces the manifestation of my healing.

John 8:36 If the Son therefore shall make you free, ye shall be free indeed.

Confession: I have been liberated and set free from the yokes of bondages of the enemy by the power of the blood of Jesus Christ. Therefore, I refuse to be bound with sickness and disease. I decree and declare my liberty in the name of Jesus Christ. I declare that I am free indeed. Satan, you can't keep me bound with this affliction because I have been set free. I exercise my liberty and freedom, and I break every chain of sickness and disease, and I declare my freedom and my healing.

Is 55:11 So shall my word be that goeth forth out of my mouth: it shall not return unto me void, but it shall accomplish that which I please, and it shall prosper in the thing whereto I sent it.

Confession: The Word of the Lord is powerful and unstoppable. When God sends His Word for a purpose, it is impossible for His Word to return void or unanswered. For there is no force or power in the heavens or the earth that can stop or even hinder God's Word from coming to pass. And, as He has spoken His Word concerning my healing, it must strike the mark and prosper me in the manifestation of my healing; for the Word of the Lord has declared it.

Ps 23:1 ...The LORD is my shepherd; I shall not want.

Confession: The Lord is my Shepherd. He supplies everything I need according to His riches in glory. He does not allow me to suffer lack, nor does He allow me to be in need or want. As my great Shepherd, He is faithful to watch over me and supply all things for me when I am in need. As I am in need of healing, the Lord is my good Shepherd who shall provide it for me. Surely, He shall not leave me in want concerning my healing.

1 John 4:4 Ye are of God, little children, and have overcome them: because greater is he that is in you, than he that is in the world.

Confession: I am a child of God. I have been born of the Spirit of God. God is alive in me and full of power. God is infinitely bigger and greater than Satan. God is also infinitely bigger and greater than any sickness or disease. Greater is Jesus Christ who lives and dwells within me — who is full of the power of God to heal and deliver me from this infirmity — than the enemy that is in the world.

Jer 8:22 Is there no balm in Gilead; is there no physician there? why then is not the health of the daughter of my people recovered?

Confession: Jesus is my Great Physician. He is the oil of the apothecary. He is the anointed One who destroys the yoke of infirmity. He is my healing oil — the balm of Gilead, my healer, and the source of my health.

Exodus 15:25 And he cried unto the Lord; and the Lord shewed him a tree, which when he had cast into the waters, the waters were made sweet...

Confession: God instructed Moses to cast the tree into the bitter waters, and the waters became sweet (pleasant and drinkable). God has likewise placed the cross of Jesus Christ into the bitter situation of my infirmity. And just as the tree (which represents the cross) changed the bitter waters into sweetness for Moses and the Israelites, I confess and decree that the bitter waters of my infirmity shall also be made sweet (which is health, wholeness, and healing).

> *John 1:1, 14 In the beginning was the Word, and the Word was with God, and the Word was God... And the Word was made flesh, and dwelt among us, (and we beheld his glory, the glory as of the only begotten of the Father,) full of grace and truth.*

Confession: Jesus is the living Word. He is the spoken Word of God. He is the Word that was in the beginning. He is the Word that became flesh and dwelled among us. He is the Glory of God, the only begotten of the Father. He is the manifested Word of God. By the power and authority of God, I release the power of the Word of God concerning my healing to become manifested in my body.

> *Luke 13:11-13 And, behold, there was a woman which had a spirit of infirmity eighteen years, and was bowed together, and could in no wise lift up herself. And when Jesus saw her, he called her to him, and said unto her, Woman, thou art loosed from thine infirmity. And he laid his hands on her: and immediately she was made straight, and glorified God.*

Confession: Jesus has declared me to be loosed and made whole. I am therefore no longer bound by this infirmity. The Word of God has loosed me, healed me, set me free, and made me whole. Satan is therefore helpless, powerless, and inoperative to continue to put sickness upon me because I have been set free. I am set free. I am whole. I am well, and I am delivered by the liberating power of the Word of God.

> *Exodus 15:26 If thou wilt diligently hearken to the voice of the Lord thy God, and wilt do that which is right in his sight, and wilt give ear to his commandments, and keep all his statutes, I will put none of these diseases upon thee, which I have brought upon the Egyptians: for I am the Lord that healeth thee.*

Confession: Egypt represents the world. The sicknesses and diseases of Egypt represents those that are in this world. Through Christ, God has delivered me from the sins of Egypt (the sins of this world). Through Christ, God has also delivered me from the sicknesses and diseases of Egypt (the sicknesses and diseases that are in this world). He is Jehovah-Rapha, the Lord who heals me, and the Lord who takes sickness and disease away from me.

> *Ps 34:19 Many are the afflictions of the righteous: but the LORD delivereth him out of them all.*

Confession: Because I am a child of God, it does not exclude me from going through afflictions. The Lord has said that the righteous would go through many afflictions, but God has promised to deliver us from them all. By God's grace, He has made me to be righteous in Christ Jesus. Therefore, I claim and receive the promise of His deliverance from this affliction, according to the promise of His Word to deliver me.

> *Galatians 2:20 I am crucified with Christ: nevertheless I live; yet not I, but Christ liveth in me: and the life which I now live in the flesh I live by the faith of the Son of God, who loved me, and gave himself for me.*

Confession: I was crucified with Christ and died with Him. As He died to sickness and disease, I too died with Him to sickness and disease. Now, Christ is risen from the dead. He has risen without sickness and disease. And, I declare that I am risen without sickness and disease because He now lives within me. And the life that I now live, I live it by my faith in His resurrected power and His healing anointing.

> *Malachi 4:2 But unto you that fear my name shall the Sun of righteousness arise with healing in his wings; and ye shall go forth, and grow up as calves of the stall.*

Confession: Jesus Christ, the Son of God, our righteousness, has risen. He has risen with all power in His hands. Through the cross, He has conquered Satan and sickness. As I speak His Word and look unto Him, He arises unto me with divine, anointed, yoke-breaking healing power in His wings.

> Ps 105:37 *He brought them forth also with silver and gold: and there was not one feeble person among their tribes.*

Confession: The Lord delivered millions of His people out of Egypt by His outstretched Hand. Before bringing them out, He also healed every single one of them. There was not one person left feeble or sick among them. He healed them all. He is the same God with the same power who heals and delivers millions today. I declare that just as God healed every one of His people and brought them out of the bondage of Egypt, He is the same God who is healing millions now and bringing them out of their infirmities. He is also the same God who is healing me now and bringing me out of this bondage of infirmity.

> 2 Ki 4:25-26 *So she went and came unto [Elisha] the man of God to mount Carmel. And it came to pass, when the man of God saw her afar off, that he said to Gehazi his servant... Run now, I pray thee, to meet her, and say unto her, Is it well with thee? Is it well with thy husband? Is it well with the child? And she answered, It is well.*

Confession: This woman released her faith for her child's healing by declaring that *"all is well"* even in the midst of her calamity. I therefore release my faith as she did, in spite of what I see, hear, or feel regarding this infirmity; and I declare by faith that *all is well*, and I am healed in the name of Jesus Christ.

Proverbs 17:22 A merry heart doeth good like a medicine: but a broken spirit drieth the bones.

Confession: Christ is in me. It's because of Him that I have the joy of the Lord. His joy gives me peace and strength. His presence and joy are being infused in me now, working in me like medicine to heal, renew, and restore my body to good health.

Joshua 6:2 And the LORD said unto Joshua, See, I have given into thine hand Jericho, and the king thereof, and the mighty men of valour.

Confession: When the walls of Jericho was still standing, God told Joshua to see by revelation his victory over Jericho and its mighty army and their great walls. God told Joshua to see this before the battle even began and before the walls came down. Joshua released his faith to see it, and God gave him the victory. God is not a respecter of persons. I likewise release my faith and I see by revelation my victory in Christ over my battle. I see by faith the walls of this infirmity coming down. And, I see myself totally healed.

2 Tim 1:7 For God hath not given us the spirit of fear; but of power, and of love, and of a sound mind.

Confession: The Lord has not given me a spirit of fear or doubt (concerning my healing), but He has given me a spirit of power, and of love, and a sound and confident mind that I shall receive the manifestation of my healing.

Luk 10:30 ...A certain man went down from Jerusalem to Jericho, and fell among thieves, which stripped him of his raiment, and wounded him, and departed, leaving him half dead.... But a certain Samaritan, as he journeyed, came where he was: and when he saw him, he had compassion on him, And went to him, and bound up his wounds, pouring in oil and wine, and set him on his own beast, and brought him to an inn, and took care of him.

Confession: It is Satan who is the thief. He comes and attempts to strip us of our healing. He comes to injure us and wound us with sickness and disease. But Jesus Christ, my Lord, is my loving and compassionate Savior. All of my help and deliverance comes from Him. Whenever I am wounded, I look unto the hills and call upon the Him, and He answers me and comes to my rescue. He pours into my wounds oil and wine, which is the healing virtue and anointing of His Spirit. He watches over me and cares for me until I am fully healed and recovered. The Lord is my heavenly good Samaritan. He is always good. He is always there for me, and He always helps and delivers me.

Col 3:15 And let the peace of God rule in your hearts, to the which also ye are called in one body; and be ye thankful.

Confession: I will not fret nor worry about this infirmity. I will not fear nor be dismayed. For my confidence is in the Lord. He is my healer. He shall not fail to heal and deliver me. Until my complete healing is manifested, I will let the peace of God strengthen and settle my heart in His peace.

Gen 18:14 Is any thing too hard for the LORD?...

Confession: My God is the Almighty, all-powerful, sovereign God. He created all the heavens and the earth with the power of His Word. He sustains all things by His great authority and power. There is nothing too hard for the Lord to do. There is no disease or sickness too hard for the Lord to heal or deliver. This infirmity that I face is a small, insignificant thing to the Lord. And by the finger of His great and mighty power He shall surely heal me.

Isa 40:29 He giveth power to the faint; and to them that have no might he increaseth strength.

Confession: The Lord gives me power when I am weak. And when I am sick, He gives strength to my body to be healed, and He makes me whole.

Is 59:19 ...When the enemy shall come in like a flood, the Spirit of the LORD shall lift up a standard against him.

Confession: The Lord is my help. When the enemy comes against me like a flood, the Spirit of the Lord shall rise up on my behalf and fight against my enemy. He shall raise up a mighty standard of war and utterly defeat and destroy my enemy. And, since my present enemy is this infirmity, I declare that the Lord shall utterly defeat and destroy this enemy in my life.

Jer 33:3 Call unto me, and I will answer thee, and shew thee great and mighty things, which thou knowest not.

Confession: The Lord is faithful unto His people. He is faithful unto them that call upon Him. For He has declared in His Word that when we call upon Him, He will answer us. So as I call upon the Lord concerning my healing, He is faithful to answer me and manifest His Word of healing on my behalf.

Is 54:17 No weapon that is formed against thee shall prosper; and every tongue that shall rise against thee in judgment thou shalt condemn. This is the heritage of the servants of the LORD, and their righteousness is of me, saith the LORD.

Confession: I am a servant of the Lord. God has given me His heritage and His blessings. As part of my heritage, He has declared that no weapon that the devil forms against me shall be able to prosper. God never said that weapons would not be formed against me, but He has promised me in His Word that they shall not prosper against me. He condemns and strikes down every weapon that is formed against me, which includes every physical, verbal, and spiritual weapon. He also condemns and strikes down every weapon that is formed against my health and my body. So by the authority of the name of Jesus Christ, I decree and declare this weapon of infirmity to be condemned and struck down by the Word of the Lord, and to be helpless, inoperative, and powerless to continue upon my body.

> *Gen 22:18 And in thy [Abraham] seed shall all the nations of the earth be blessed; because thou hast obeyed my voice.*

Confession: God gave Abraham a promise that He would bless Abraham and his descendents. Because of Christ, I have been made the righteousness of God, joint heirs with Christ, the seed of Abraham, and therefore heirs according to the promise. I therefore, as an heir to the promises of God, receive the promise of God's divine healing.

> *Ps 91:3 Surely he shall deliver thee from the snare of the fowler, and from the noisome pestilence.*

Confession: God delivers me from every snare, trap, and attack of the enemy. Because I put my trust in Him, He shall also deliver me from this attack against my body.

> *Is 58:6 Is not this the fast that I have chosen? to loose the bands of wickedness, to undo the heavy burdens, and to let the oppressed go free, and that ye break every yoke?*

Confession: Through the power of the Holy Ghost, God has anointed me with His anointing to destroy every yoke of the devil in my life. Therefore, by the power of God, I loose this wicked band and burden of sickness and disease from my body. I destroy every yoke that has been assigned against my body, and I decree and declare by the power of the living God, that I am healed and set free.

Is 58:8 Then shall thy light break forth as the morning, and thine health shall spring forth speedily: and thy righteousness shall go before thee; the glory of the LORD shall be thy rereward.

Confession: As I pray and confess the Word of the Lord over my life and my body, the glory of the Lord shines upon me. His glory shines upon me like the sun. Just as the sun gives and renews life and strength to all living things, the glory of the Lord strengthens and renews my life, my body, and my health. The glory of the Lord causes my healing to break forth as a new, tender plant. And, His glory causes my health to spring forth speedily, as the presence and righteousness of God goes before me. For the glory of the Lord is my reward.

James 4:10 Humble yourselves in the sight of the Lord, and he shall lift you up.

Confession: I humble myself in the sight of the Lord under His mighty hand. For He is great and greatly to be praised. As I exalt Him, He lifts me up from this place of sickness and disease. He heals my body and sets my feet upon the Rock, and restores me to good health.

James 5:14-15 Is any sick among you? Let him call for the elders of the church; and let them pray over him, anointing him with oil in the name of the Lord: And the prayer of faith shall save the sick, and the Lord shall raise him up; and if he have committed sins, they shall be forgiven him.

Confession: Whenever there is sickness or disease upon me, I call for the elders (mature men and women of God and of prayer) to join with me in prayer and anoint me with oil in the name of the Lord. As the prayer of faith is made upon my behalf, God anoints me with His healing oil of gladness. He forgives me of all of my sins and iniquities.

He removes every hindrance to my healing, and He raises me up and restores me to good health.

> *James 5:16 Confess your faults one to another, and pray one for another, that ye may be healed. The effectual fervent prayer of a righteous man availeth much.*

Confession: As I have prayed for others to be healed, the Lord is faithful to also heal my body when I pray. Through God's grace, He has made me righteous through Christ. Therefore, because of the righteousness of Christ that is upon me, my effectual, fervent prayers avail much in victory.

> *John 14:12-14 Verily, verily, I say unto you, He that believeth on me, the works that I do shall he do also; and greater works than these shall he do; because I go unto my Father. And whatsoever ye shall ask in my name, that will I do, that the Father may be glorified in the Son. If ye shall ask any thing in my name, I will do it.*

Confession: I believe in God the Father Almighty. I believe in the Lord, Jesus Christ. I believe that He died on the cross for my sins, sicknesses, and diseases. I believe in the Word of the living God. I believe that whatever I ask according to His Word, in the name of Jesus Christ, that He will do it for me. So as I have asked for my healing, I believe that it is done. And I receive my healing, in the name of Jesus Christ.

> *Eph 2:8-9 For by grace are ye saved through faith; and that not of yourselves: it is the gift of God: Not of works, lest any man should boast.*

Confession: Through the blood of Jesus Christ, God has given me G.R.A.C.E. (*God's riches at Christ's expense*). One of the many wonderful riches of the Kingdom of God is the abundant gift of healing. This wonderful gift of healing my body is not given to me by my works, nor by anything that

I have done. It is a gift from God. It is given to me by His grace through my faith in His Son, Jesus Christ.

Php 4:6 Be careful for nothing; but in every thing by prayer and supplication with thanksgiving let your requests be made known unto God.

Confession: Through my prayers and supplications, I make my requests known unto God. I give thanksgiving and praise to Him because He hears my prayers and answers them. And as I have prayed for my healing, I give thanksgiving in advance because I know that He has heard me and has sent my deliverance.

Jer 17:14 Heal me, O LORD, and I shall be healed; save me, and I shall be saved: for thou art my praise.

Confession: The Lord is my praise. He is my glory. He is the One whom I worship and magnify. Because I have set my praise and love upon Him, He shall save, deliver, and heal me from this affliction. For He alone is my God and my Lord.

Jer 33:6 Behold, I will bring [them] health and cure, and I will cure them, and will reveal unto them the abundance of peace and truth.

Confession: God is abundant in mercy, kindness, peace, and truth unto His people. Through the abundance of His grace, He will abundantly heal me; for He is the One who cures me and brings healing unto me.

And when Elisha was come into the house, behold, the child was dead... He went in therefore, and shut the door upon them twain, and prayed unto the LORD. And he went up, and lay upon the child, and put his mouth upon his mouth, and his eyes upon his eyes, and his hands upon his hands: and he stretched himself upon the child; and the flesh of the child waxed warm.... and the child sneezed seven times, and the child opened his eyes. (2Ki 4:32-36)

Confession: This child was revived by the healing power of the Almighty God. The same power that revived this child is the same power that is at work today, and it's the same power that is able to (and will) revive and heal my body.

As Elisha put his mouth on the child's mouth, I put my mouth on the Word by speaking and confessing the Word of God. As he put his eyes upon the child's eyes, I put my eyes upon the Word as I read the living Word of God. As He put his hands on the child's hands, I reach forth by faith and touch the Lord with my hands in faith. As I steadfastly do these things, the Lord covers my body with His healing anointing just as Elisha covered this child with his body. And, as this child was miraculously raised by the healing power of God, I shall also be raised from this affliction by the same, never-changing, never-failing, anointed power of the Living God.

Mar 9:23-24 Jesus said unto him, If thou canst believe, all things are possible to him that believeth. And straightway the father of the child cried out, and said with tears, Lord, I believe; help thou mine unbelief.

Confession: I believe in Jesus Christ our Lord and Savior. I believe that He is the Son of God--the living Word of God, who was manifested in the earth and among men. Jesus has declared that as a believer, all things are possible to me. Therefore I declare that healing is for me. I also declare that since I am in Christ, that I receive and stand upon the faith of Christ. And, it's the faith of Christ that helps my unbelief. His faith compensates and covers my unbelief and lack of faith. Therefore it's because of His faith I stand in full assurance that I shall receive my healing.

John1:5 And the light shineth in darkness; and the darkness comprehended it not.

Confession: Jesus is the Light of the world. Sickness and disease is of the darkness of this world. As I speak and confess the Word of God concerning my healing, the light of Jesus Christ shines upon the spirit of darkness (sickness and disease) and disbands it from me. Therefore, I declare that the power of the darkness of this spirit of infirmity is broken from by body. And, because of the everlasting light of the Word of God, this spirit of darkness shall not be able to return.

Ps 118:8 It is better to trust in the LORD than to put confidence in man.

Confession: I thank God for giving me doctors and medicine. But even though God may use them to help me, I put my trust and confidence in the Lord. God is my cure and my healer from my infirmities; therefore, my praise belongs to Him. He gets all the glory for my healing because it is the Lord who ultimately heals me. Regardless of which source He uses, it is He who cures me and brings health to my body.

Job 22:28 Thou shalt also decree a thing, and it shall be established unto thee: and the light shall shine upon thy ways.

Confession: I am a king unto the Most High King, Jesus Christ. Where the word of a king is, there is power. So by the power and authority of the Most High King, Jesus Christ, I decree and declare my healing to be established and manifested in my body.

Job 33:25 His flesh shall be fresher than a child's: he shall return to the days of his youth.

Confession: My God is the God of restoration. He restores my soul. He redeems my life from destruction. He renews my life, health, and strength like the eagle. He satisfies me with His good blessings. And, as I pray and confess the

Word of God over my body, my health shall be restored and renewed like that of a child.

> *Act 3:6 Then Peter said, silver and gold have I none; but such as I have give I thee: In the name of Jesus Christ of Nazareth rise up and walk.*

Confession: There is power in the name of Jesus Christ. Demons tremble and flee at the mere sound of His name. In the name of Jesus Christ, the lame walk, the blind see, the sick are healed, and the dead are raised. In the name of Jesus Christ, I command my body to rise up from this place of affliction and be healed!

> *Mat 16:19 And I will give unto thee the keys of the kingdom of heaven: and whatsoever thou shalt bind on earth shall be bound in heaven: and whatsoever thou shalt loose on earth shall be loosed in heaven.*

Confession: Through Christ Jesus, God has given unto me the keys of the Kingdom of Heaven. He has declared that whatever I bind or loose in the physical or spiritual realm shall be bound and loosed. Therefore, I bind this affliction in the physical and the spiritual realm, and I loose its hold and power to afflict my body. And, by the authority of the power of the keys to the Kingdom, I decree and declare that I am loosed, set free, and healed.

> *1 Cor 15:57 But thanks be to God, which giveth us the victory through our Lord Jesus Christ.*

Confession: I give thanks unto my God who has given me the victory over all things in the name of our Lord, Jesus Christ. I therefore claim my victory. I stand in my place of victory. I walk in my place of victory; and I declare my victory over this infirmity, in the name of Jesus Christ.

> *Ex 3:13 And Moses said unto God, Behold, when I come unto the children of Israel… and they shall say to*

me, What is his name? what shall I say unto them? And God said unto Moses, I AM THAT I AM: and he said, Thus shalt thou say unto the children of Israel, I AM hath sent me unto you.

Confession: My God is the Great *I AM THAT I AM*. I AM means that He is All-powerful, He has All-authority, He has All-dominion, and He is the Almighty God. I AM means that He is the source and sustainer of all things. I AM means that He alone deserves all the praise and all the glory. I AM also means that He is whatever we need. And, since I need Him to be my healer, for me, I AM means that He is Jehovah-Rapha, the Lord who is my healer.

Lk 6:19 And the whole multitude sought to touch him: for there went virtue out of him, and healed them all.

Confession: Jesus is the living Word of God. God's Word contains healing virtue. As I speak the Word of God concerning my healing, the virtue of the Lord is stirred, activated, and released upon my life and my body, which produces the manifestation of my healing.

John 10:10 The thief cometh not, but for to steal, and to kill, and to destroy: I am come that they might have life, and that they might have it more abundantly.

Confession: The thief comes to steal, kill, and destroy my health. But he shall not be able to prosper against me because the Lord has rebuked the devourer for my sake. Therefore, Satan cannot destroy my health, and neither can He continue to bring any sickness or disease upon me. For God has given me His abundant life of wholeness and healing.

Pro 16:24 Pleasant words are as an honeycomb, sweet to the soul, and health to the bones.

Confession: I will cling to the Word of God. I will eat and feast off His Word daily. His Word is pleasant to every part of my being. His Word is sweeter than the honey in a honeycomb. His Word gives peace to my mind, comfort to my soul, and encouragement to my heart. His Word also heals me from the crown of my head to the soles of my feet. His Word gives health to my bones and heals and restores every fiber of my flesh.

> *Mark 11:23 For verily I say unto you, that whosoever shall say unto this mountain, be thou removed, and be thou cast into the sea; and shall not doubt in his heart, but shall believe that those things which he saith shall come to pass; he shall have whatsoever he saith.*

Confession: God has given me power and authority to speak to my mountains. So by the authority that He has given unto me through Christ Jesus, I command each and every mountain of sickness, disease, and spirit of infirmity to be completely removed from my body and cast into the sea. I do not doubt the Word of God concerning my healing. I believe that I have already received it. Therefore, I shall have what I have spoken.

> *Mat 21:19 And when he saw a fig tree in the way, he came to it, and found nothing thereon, but leaves only, and said unto it, Let no fruit grow on thee henceforward for ever. And presently the fig tree withered away.*

Confession: As Jesus cursed the fig tree and told it to die, it died. Jesus has also given me the same authority; therefore, I curse this sickness and disease from my body, and I command it to wither, dry up, and die at the roots. And, as the fig tree ceased to live after Jesus cursed it, I decree that as I have cursed this sickness, that it shall also cease to dwell upon my body.

> *Num 23:19 God is not a man, that he should lie; neither the son of man, that he should repent: hath he said, and shall he not do it? or hath he spoken, and shall he not*

make it good?

Confession: God is not like a mere, mortal man. For as high as the highest heavens are above the earth, so is the Lord above man. For man speaks and tells lies and must repent for the failure of his words. But the Word of the Lord cannot fail. His Word divinely unstoppable. Whatever the Lord speaks comes to pass. His Word cannot be stopped or hindered by any power or force in the universe. Therefore, the Lord shall make good the Word of healing that He has spoken concerning my body.

Php 1:6 Being confident of this very thing, that he which hath begun a good work in you will perform it until the day of Jesus Christ:

Confession: I am confident in the Word of the Lord. I am also confident in the finished work of the Lord. And, as the Lord has begun the work of healing in my body, He will not leave it undone. He will finish the work and complete the process of healing in which He has begun.

Pro 15:29 The LORD is far from the wicked: but he heareth the prayer of the righteous.

Confession: The Lord does not hear the prayers of those who are against Him and those who are not in covenant with Him. But for His covenant children who love Him, and those who are made righteous through Jesus Christ, He readily and anxiously hears their prayers and answers them.

Rom 4:17 (As it is written, I have made thee a father of many nations,) before him whom he believed, even God, who quickeneth the dead, and calleth those things which be not as though they were.

Confession: I am a person of faith. I walk by faith. I live by faith. I see by faith. And by my faith, I call those things that be not as though they were. Therefore, even though I do not see my healing in the physical realm, I see it by faith in the spiritual realm. I say that it is already done. I say that I am already healed. For I speak by faith and boldly declare that the Lord has already quickened and healed my body.

Rom 4:21 And being fully persuaded that, what he had promised, he was able also to perform.

Confession: I am fully persuaded in the Lord and in the promises of His Word. I bind and cast down all doubt from my heart, mind, and soul concerning my healing. And, I stand fully persuaded and in full assurance that what the Lord has promised me in His Word concerning my healing, He is well able to, and He will perform.

Rom 8:31 What shall we then say to these things? If God be for us, who can be against us?

Confession: I was once the enemy of God through sin and disobedience. But the chastisement of my peace with God was laid upon Jesus when He took the stripes for me. Because of His sufferings, I have been made a friend of God, and I am now favored by Him. Because of Christ, God is now with me. And, since God is for me and with me, there is no sickness or disease that can prosper against my body, and there is no spirit or force that can keep me from receiving my healing.

Exodus 23:25 And ye shall serve the Lord your God, and he shall bless thy bread, and thy water; and I will take sickness away from the midst of thee.

Confession: As I serve the Lord, my God, He is faithful unto His Word. As I speak His Word, He blesses it and causes the blessings of His Word to be manifested in my life. He also blesses the manifestation of His Word concerning my healing. For He removes sickness and disease from my body and casts it far from me.

Ps 91:15 He shall call upon me, and I will answer him: I will be with him in trouble; I will deliver him, and honour him.

Confession: The Lord is nigh unto His people and hears their cry in times of distress. For when I am in trouble, the Lord has declared that I can call upon Him and He will answer me. Therefore, because of my affliction, I look unto Him and call upon His holy name. And, because of His faithfulness to His Word, He will answer me, deliver me, and heal me.

Ps 91:16 With long life will I satisfy him, and shew him my salvation.

Confession: My God is faithful unto His Word. He has promised me a long life. And, He is faithful to fulfill His promise to bless me with a long life. Because of His faithfulness, I decree and declare according to His Word that I shall live a long and healthy life, as He blesses me and shows me the manifestation of His great salvation.

Rom 8:11 But if the Spirit of him that raised up Jesus from the dead dwell in you, he that raised up Christ from the dead shall also quicken your mortal bodies by his Spirit that dwelleth in you.

Confession: With God's awesome power, He raised up Christ from the dead. He is now living within me. And, it's that same spirit that is alive within me that quickens and heals my body and raises me up from this affliction. I therefore declare that I am risen and healed by the quickening power of God through Jesus Christ.

Eze 16:6 And when I passed by thee, and saw thee polluted in thine own blood, I said unto thee when thou wast in thy blood, <u>Live</u>; yea, I said unto thee when thou wast in thy blood, <u>Live</u>.

Confession: The Lord is the source of all life. His Word contains the Zoe power and life of God. The Lord has given me His authority to speak and release the power and life of His Word. Therefore, I speak and release Zoe life and health to my body. I command my body to arise from this place of affliction. And, I command it to be strengthened and healed, in the name of the Lord.

Heb 4:15 For we have not an high priest which cannot be touched with the feeling of our infirmities; but was in all points tempted like as we are, yet without sin.

Confession: Jesus Christ is my heavenly High Priest. He is not a high priest that is unreachable or untouchable. He can relate to all the things we go through. He knows our pains. He feels our infirmities. For He was tempted in all things as we are, but He overcame all temptations and tests. He now sits on the right hand of God the Father making intercessions for me. Because He is my High Priest who intercedes for me, I shall receive my victory over this infirmity, and I shall be healed.

Job 1:10 Hast not thou made an hedge about him, and about his house, and about all that he hath on every side? thou hast blessed the work of his hands, and his substance is increased in the land.

Confession: The Lord surrounds me with His hedge of protection. He covers and protects me on every side and in every area of my life. His angels are encamped in a hedge of protection around me continually. He not only protects me from physical hurt, harm, and danger, He also protects my body from sickness and disease.

Pro 3:8 It shall be health to thy navel, and marrow to thy bones.

Confession: The Word of the Lord is the source of my life and the strength of my heart. I live, move, and have my being in Him. He is my Daily Bread. He feeds and nourishes me with the vitality of His Word. As an unborn baby draws its nourishment and life through the umbilical cord from its mother, I also draw nourishment from the life-giving power of the Word of God. His Word heals and restores every part of my spirit, soul, and my body. That includes every cell, molecule, tissue, organ, and every part of my body even to the marrow of my bones.

> *Heb 4:12 For the word of God is quick, and powerful, and sharper than any two-edged sword, piercing even to the dividing asunder of soul and spirit, and of the joints and marrow, and is a discerner of the thoughts and intents of the heart.*

Confession: The Word of God is alive, awesome, and powerful. It is sharper than a two-edged sword. It pierces and separates things deep within us. It brings conviction and changes to the soul, and it brings enlightenment and strength to the spirit. Like a surgeon's knife, it cuts to the inner core of our being. It examines the heart and motives and discerns its inner intent. And as I speak the Word of God, it also goes deep into my body and soul and completely cuts out this infirmity.

> *Ps 118:17 I shall not die, but live, and declare the works of the LORD.*

Confession: The Lord's grace and blessings are upon me to live long, prosper, and be in good health. Therefore, I stand upon the promises of God that I shall not die of this infirmity; nor shall I continue in this affliction any longer. I shall live a long and healthy life, and I shall declare the mighty works of the Lord.

> *Ps 121:1-2 ...I will lift up mine eyes unto the hills, from whence cometh my help. My help cometh from the LORD, which made heaven and earth.*

Confession: In my time of affliction, I will look up and I will keep my eyes and my hope upon the Lord. He is the One who has made the heavens and the earth. He sustains and renews all things by His power and might. It is He who is the source of my help (and my healing). For my help (healing and deliverance) comes from the Lord.

> *Ps 138:8 The LORD will perfect that which concerneth me: thy mercy, O LORD, endureth for ever: forsake not the works of thine own hands.*

Confession: The Lord will perfect (take care of, deliver me from, and heal me of) the things that concern me. And since this affliction concerns me, the Lord shall heal and deliver me. For the Lord will not forsake His mercy toward me. And, He shall not forsake the promise of His Word concerning my deliverance.

> *2Ki 20:1-6 ...Hezekiah [was] sick unto death.... Then he turned his face to the wall, and prayed unto the LORD, saying, I beseech thee, O LORD, remember now how I have walked before thee in truth and with a perfect heart, and have done that which is good in thy sight.... [then] the word of the LORD came to [Isaiah], saying... Thus saith the LORD, the God of David thy father, I have heard thy prayer, I have seen thy tears: behold, I will heal thee...*

Confession: Hezekiah was healed because he turned his face to the wall in prayer and sought the Lord. In his prayer he reminded God of his own righteousness. I live under a much better covenant than Hezekiah. Because of the cross, I am fully covered and clothed with the righteousness of Jesus Christ. So instead of my righteousness, I remind God of Jesus' righteousness. I therefore decree and declare that it is by the righteousness of Jesus Christ that the Lord hears and answers my prayer, and He heals my body.

> *Ps 146:8 The LORD openeth the eyes of the blind: the*

LORD raiseth them that are bowed down: the LORD loveth the righteous.

Confession: The Lord loves His people. He loves those who are made righteous in Him though Christ. He has pity and compassion on those who are sick. He therefore heals, raises up, and opens the eyes of His people who are bowed down with affliction. And, because He loves me, He shall raise me up and heal me.

Mar 2:4-11 And when they could not come nigh unto him for the press, they uncovered the roof where he was: and when they had broken it up, they let down the bed wherein the sick of the palsy lay. When Jesus saw their faith, he said unto the sick of the palsy, Son, thy sins be forgiven thee.... Arise, and take up thy bed, and go thy way into thine house.

Confession: Jesus is our healer. He looks for those who would reach out by faith and believe and receive His divine healing. When He saw the faith of these men, He spoke and released power for this man to be forgiven and healed. Jesus is also looking at me now. As I stand in faith in Him and in His Word, He sees my faith, and the faith, prayers, and intercession of others who are praying and interceding on my behalf. He therefore forgives me of all my sins, and rewards our faith with His grace of divine healing for me.

Mat 28:18 And Jesus came and spake unto them, saying, All power is given unto me in heaven and in earth.

Confession: All power and authority has been given unto the Lord Jesus Christ. He is still healing the sick by the same awesome power that He did over two thousand years ago. And He is yet healing me now by His same great power.

Ps 23:3-4 He restoreth my soul: he leadeth me in the paths of righteousness for his name's sake. Yea, though I walk through the valley of the shadow of death, I will fear no evil: for thou art with me; thy rod and thy staff they comfort me.

Confession: It is the Lord who restores my soul and my body when I am sick. He leads me in the paths of His righteousness for His namesake. Even when I walk through the valley and the shadow of affliction, I will fear no evil, for the Lord is with me. His Word and His presence shall comfort and heal me.

Ps 27:14 Wait on the LORD: be of good courage, and he shall strengthen thine heart: wait, I say, on the LORD.

Confession: I will wait patiently upon the Lord. I will not doubt the Lord concerning my healing. I will continue to renew my faith in the strength of His Word. As I wait upon the Lord, I will be of good courage, and He shall strengthen my heart and heal my body.

Ps 30:2 O LORD my God, I cried unto thee, and thou hast healed me.

Confession: In my distress, I called upon the LORD and cried unto Him. He heard my voice out of His temple, and my cry came before Him, *even* into His ears. The Lord is gracious and merciful unto His people who cry unto Him. As I have cried out unto the Lord concerning my healing, He has heard my cry, and He is even now helping me, delivering me, and healing me.

Eph 6:10 Finally, my brethren, be strong in the Lord, and in the power of his might.

Confession: I confess that through Christ, God has made me to be strong in Him and in the power of His might. God has made me strong through the strength of His name and the power and strength of His Word. Through Christ, He has given me strength and soundness in my mind, strength and peace in my soul, and strength in my body.

Ps 55:22 Cast thy burden upon the LORD, and he shall sustain thee: he shall never suffer the righteous to be moved.

Confession: It is the Lord who sustains the heavens and the earth and all that is therein. For He alone is the Lord. And by His great power and might, He upholds all things. Therefore, I cast this burden of affliction upon Him. And, just as He has the power to sustain the universe, He has the power to sustain me through my affliction until my change and deliverance come.

Ps 73:26 My flesh and my heart faileth: but God is the strength of my heart, and my portion for ever.

Confession: Man will fail. The things of this world will fail. And I may fail in my flesh and my heart. But there is one truth that will always prevail: God will never fail, because there is no failure in God. God is my strength, my rock, and my fortress. He alone is my healer, and surely He shall not fail to heal me.

Mark 11:24 Therefore I say unto you, What things soever ye desire, when ye pray, believe that ye receive them, and ye shall have them.

Confession: I am a believer. I walk by my faith in God and in His Word and not by sight. I release my faith now, and I believe by faith that as I have prayed for my healing, that I have already received it, therefore, I shall have the manifestation of my healing.

Act 1:8 But ye shall receive power, after that the Holy Ghost is come upon you: and ye shall be witnesses unto me both in Jerusalem, and in all Judaea, and in Samaria, and unto the uttermost part of the earth.

Confession: God has given me the authority and power of the Holy Ghost. For He has filled me with the Holy Ghost. Therefore, I speak and release the power of the Holy Ghost, and I decree and declare my body to be healed, in the name of Jesus Christ.

Philippians 2:13 For it is God which worketh in you both to will and to do of his good pleasure.

Confession: It is the Lord's *good pleasure* to give unto me His bountiful blessings. His healing virtue is at work in me, healing and delivering me from this infirmity.

Gen 1:26 And God said, Let us make man in our image, after our likeness: and let them have dominion over the fish of the sea, and over the fowl of the air, and over the cattle, and over all the earth, and over every creeping thing that creepeth [lives or moves] upon the earth.

Confession: I am a child of God. I walk in God's power, authority and dominion. It is through Jesus Christ that God has given me authority over every creature that lives and moves upon the earth. And, since bacteria, germs, fungus, viruses and cancers are living organisms that move and grow, they fall under the divine authority that God has given unto me over them through Christ. Therefore, through the name of Jesus Christ, I take authority over every living, moving, creeping, harmful organism in my body. As Jesus cursed the fig tree and told it to die, I therefore curse every harmful organism in my body and command it to die at the very root and cease to exist in or on my body. And, by the authority and power of Jesus Christ, I decree that I am whole, healthy and healed.

Phil 1:3 Blessed be the God and Father of our Lord Jesus Christ, who hath blessed us with all spiritual blessings in heavenly places in Christ:

Confession: All blessings, all praises, all honor, and all glory be unto God, the Father of our Lord, Jesus Christ. For He has given us spiritual blessings in heavenly places. They are given to us through Christ. For we are in Him. And, in Him I receive the abundant blessings of the Kingdom of heaven which includes the grace of God for my divine healing.

> *1 Sam 14:6 And Jonathan said... the LORD will work for us: for there is no restraint to the LORD to save by many or by few.*

Confession: The Lord is my deliverer. He is my healer. There is no restraint for the Lord to heal me. Whether He heals me through the doctors and medicines or through His miraculous power, He is still my healer. And, He deserves the glory and praise for my healing.

> *Acts 28:27 ...Least thy should see with heir eyes, and hear with their ears, and understand with their heart, and should be converted, and I should heal them.*

Confession: My heart, mind, and soul are like rich, watered soil, prepared to receive the seed of God's Word. My eyes are anointed to see, my ears are anointed to hear, and my heart is anointed to receive the faith, power, and anointing of God's Word that releases life and the abundance of God's grace to heal my body.

> *Is 41:10 Fear thou not; for I am with thee: be not dismayed; for I am thy God: I will strengthen thee; yea, I will help thee; yea, I will uphold thee with the right hand of my righteousness.*

Confession: I will not fear nor be dismayed because of this infirmity. For the Lord, my God, is with me. He shall strengthen my body. He shall help and deliver me. And, He shall surely lift me up from this affliction and heal me with the right hand of His power.

> *Mal 3:11 And I will rebuke the devourer for your sakes, and he shall not destroy the fruits of your ground; neither shall your vine cast her fruit before the time in the field, saith the LORD of hosts.*

Confession: The Lord is my deliverer. He rebukes the devourer from my life and my body for the sake of the cross and the sacrifice of Jesus Christ. The Lord has also given me power and authority to rebuke the devourer. Therefore, I rebuke Satan, as well as sickness and disease from touching my body. I also rebuke every negative report of doctors and anything or anyone else that would attempt to come against my healing. And, I declare that Satan cannot destroy the fruit of my life (which is my health). Instead, the Lord gives me good health; for He is the Lord of hosts.

Rom 12:3 For I say, through the grace given unto me... according as God hath dealt to every man <u>the measure of faith</u>.

Confession: As a believer, God has given each of us the measure of faith. There is faith on the inside of me to be healed. As I speak and confess God's Word, the measure of faith that God has given me on the inside is transformed from my spirit and is manifested in my body, and I am healed.

Mat 6:13 And lead us not into temptation, but deliver us from evil: For thine is the kingdom, and the power, and the glory, for ever. Amen.

Confession: In the name of Jesus Christ, I decree and declare that I am healed. For Yours, O LORD, is the Kingdom, and the power, and the glory, forever and ever. And for my salvation, the wondrous blessings that You have bestowed upon me, and for my divine healing, I say to You, O Lord my God, be all the Glory. AMEN.

Other Biblical Ways of Receiving Divine Healing

God has given us many keys in which we can receive our healing and blessings. We are to utilize every key that God has made accessible to us. The following are some additional keys that you may utilize:

1. Through the Laying on of Hands:

And these signs shall follow them that believe; In my name shall they cast out devils; they shall speak with new tongues; They shall take up serpents; and if they drink any deadly thing, it shall not hurt them; they shall lay hands on the sick, and they shall recover. Mar 16:17-18

2. Through Praying and Confessing the Word:

For verily I say unto you, That whosoever shall say unto this mountain, Be thou removed, and be thou cast into the sea; and shall not doubt in his heart, but shall believe that those things which he saith shall come to pass; he shall have whatsoever he saith. Mar 11:23

3. Through Fasting and Payer:

And when he was come into the house, his disciples asked him privately, Why could not we cast him out? And he said unto them, This kind can come forth by nothing, but by prayer and fasting. Mar 9:28-29

4. Through Anointing with Oil:

Is any sick among you? let him call for the elders of the church; and let them pray over him, anointing him with oil in the name of the Lord: And the prayer of faith shall save the sick, and the Lord shall raise him up; and if he have committed sins, they shall be forgiven him. James 5:14-15

5. Through Touching and Agreeing:

Again I say unto you, That if two of you shall agree on earth as touching any thing that they shall ask, it shall be done for them of my Father which is in heaven. For where two or three are gathered together in my name, there am I in the midst of them. Mat 18:19-20

6. Through Praying for Others:

Give, and it shall be given unto you; good measure, pressed down, and shaken together, and running over, shall men give into your bosom. For with the same measure that ye mete withal it shall be measured to you again. Luke 6:38

7. Through Medicine:

Drink no longer water, but use a little wine for thy stomach's sake and thine often infirmities. 1 Ti 5:23

In this passage Paul was advising Timothy to drink a little wine for his stomach ailment. Paul was not advocating social drinking, but rather, using wine as a probiotic medicine for his stomach issues.

In the Name of Jesus Christ

And whatsoever ye shall ask in my name, that will I do, that the Father may be glorified in the Son. If ye shall ask any thing in my name, I will do it. John 14:13-14

The above are seven ways in which we can receive our healing. Regardless of whether you use one, some, or all of the above methods, they must be done in the Name of Jesus Christ. It's the power and authority of His name that produces the power to be healed.

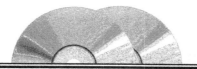

Decreeing your Healing Is Available Now on CD

This 2 CD series contains the powerful spiritual warfare healing confessions and declarations that are in this book. They are narrated by the author, Kenneth Scott.

Allow the healing Word of God to saturate your mind, soul, and body with God's healing anointing, as you drive in your car or sit in your home and meditate on God's Word.

14.99
Confessions only. Not the entire book

Other Books By Kenneth Scott

The Weapons Of Our Warfare, Volume 1
This is a handbook of scriptural based prayers for just about every need in your life. There are prayers for your home, marriage, family and many personal issues that we face in our lives each day. If you desire to be developed in prayer, then this is a must book for you.

The Weapons Of Our Warfare, Volume 2
This handbook is a sequel of Volume I, and brings the prayer warrior into the ministry of intercession. It has prayers for your church, pastor, city, our nation, and many other national issues for which we should pray. If you desire to be developed as an intercessor, then this book is for you.

The Weapons Of Our Warfare, Volume 3
(Confessing God's Word Over Your Life)
There is a difference between prayer and confession. This book gives the believer understanding about confessions and what they do in your life. It also contains daily confessions for major areas of your life. If you have Volumes 1 and 2, then you also need Volume 3.

The Weapons Of Our Warfare Volumes 1 ,2 & 3 on CD
Meditate on the Word of God as it is prayed on audio CDs. These CDs contain prayers from Volumes 1 2, & 3 (sold separately). As you hear these prayers prayed, you can stand in the spirit of agreement and apply them in the spirit to your life, situations and circumstances as you ride in your car or sit at home. In the Volume 3 Confession series, Pastor Scott will lead you in confessions, allowing you to easily follow and quote them afterwards. These CDs are a must for every Christian library.

The Weapons Of Our Warfare, Volume 4
(Prayers for Teens and Young Adults)
Teenagers have different needs than adults. This is a prayer handbook that keeps the same fervency and fire as Volumes 1 & 2, but also addresses the needs of teens. This book is a must for your teens.

The Weapons Of Our Warfare, Volume 5
Through the warfare of "praise and worship," this book teaches you how to go on the assault against the forces of darkness and tear Satan's kingdom down in your life and circumstances. Psalm 68:1 tells us that when God arises, the enemy becomes scattered. When you praise, you raise! In other words, when you praise and worship God, He begins to rise up on you, in you, in your presence, your surroundings, and even in your situations and circumstances. Since the enemy cannot stand God's presence, he has to scatter and flee, releasing and leaving your stuff behind.

The Witchcraft of Profanity
When people use profanity, they think they are simply speaking empty, vain words. These words are not vain at all. They are actually witchcraft spells, evoking demon spirits upon their life and the lives of those they speak over. Get this book for yourself

and for others, and learn what's actually going on in the spiritual realm when profanity is used. Once you read this book, you will never use profanity again!

When All Hell Breaks Loose
Most mature Christians can survive a casual trial here and there, but many of God's people fall during the storms of life. Get this book and learn how to prevail through the storm, *"When all Hell Breaks Loose."*

Praying in Your Divine Authority
Many Christians are hindered and defeated by Satan simply because they do not know the dominion and authority they have in Christ. This book teaches the believer how to bind and loose Satan and demon spirits, and how to pray and walk in our divine authority.

The Warfare of Fasting
Jesus said that some spiritual strongholds, hindrances and bondages will only be broken through prayer and fasting. This book teaches the believer the different types of fasts, the methods of fasting, and the warfare of what happens in the spiritual realm when we fast. If you want to see "total" deliverance in your life, you need to get this book.

Standing In The Gap
In this book Pastor Scott teaches life-changing principles of what it means to make up the hedge, stand in the gap, stand in agreement, and intercede for others. If you are a prayer warrior, an intercessor, or you have a desire to be one, this book is a must for you.

Too Blessed to be Cursed
Do generational curses actually exist? Where do they come from? Does God send generational curses upon my life, or are they from the devil? Could it be that some of my difficulties and struggles in life come from generational curses? If there is a curse on my life or family, can it be broken? Using the life of David, Pastor Scott answers these and other questions about generational curses and teaches you how to get set free and receive your deliverance from generational curses by blood of Jesus Christ.

The Basics of Prayer —Understanding The Lord's Prayer
Just about all of us have prayed "The Lord's Prayer," and even know The Lord's Prayer by memory. But very few of us really understand the depths of what Jesus was truly teaching His disciples in this prayer outline. This book gives the believer a scripture by scripture breakdown of this prayer and gives illumination and insight on its understanding.

Why We Act Like That!
Pastor Scott traces the root cause of many African-American issues of today to the spirit of slavery. He parallels the problems the Children of Israel had with post-Egyptian bondage to issues African-Americans now face in the post-slavery era. He shows us that there is a slavery mindset that is still influencing many of the issues that African-Americans deal with to this very day. He also shows us how we can overcome them through the power of God, His Word, and deliverance.

Order at: prayerwarfare.com

Contact Us:

For prayer requests, questions or comments, write to:

Spiritual Warfare Ministries
Attention: Kenneth Scott
P.O. Box 2024
Birmingham, Alabama 35201-2024

(205) 853-9509

Web Site:

www.prayerwarfare.com
or
www.spiritualwarfare.cc

email us at prayerbooks@aol.com

This book is not available in all bookstores. To order additional copies of this book, you may order at our website above, or you may do so by sending $11.99 plus $2.98 shipping and handling to the above address.